We often neglect one of God's primary sources of what we need: human relationships. Townsend teaches us a biblical, practical, and research-supported path to providing for, and being provided for by, the right people.

—ANDY STANLEY, senior pastor, North
Point Community Church; author

Townsend provides a guide for cultivating the relationships that help us reach our potential and pour into the lives of those around us. An essential read for optimizing the relationships in our lives to be our best, most life-giving selves.

—SHANNON SEDGWICK DAVIS, president and
CEO, Bridgeway Foundation; author

Townsend reminds us that all roads lead to healthy, vibrant, and life-giving relationships, a truth I wish I had leaned into in my formative years as a leader, when I had a PhD in achievement but was at a third-grade level in people. *People Fuel* helps us to skip a few grades.

—BRYAN LORITTS, author, *Insider/Outsider*

In a world where it's so easy to isolate and hide behind our phones, this book is incredibly valuable. We know that relationships matter, but now we've got a blueprint to how to build the right ones.

—JON ACUFF, author, *New York Times* bestselling
Finish: Give Yourself the Gift of Done

Healthy relationships are hard to maintain. I'm thankful for discerning guides like John Townsend who give us the tools and insights to foster life-giving relationships.

—GABE LYONS, president, Q Ideas; author, *Good Faith*

We often forget that God provides for our needs through relationships. John teaches us about the life-giving nutrients that come through necessary relationships and instructs us on how to develop the ones we lack.

—GREG BRENNEMAN, former CEO, Continental
Airlines, Burger King, Quizno's and CCMP

In his compelling new book, John Townsend examines the ways that our relationships shape us into flourishing, productive people. And as we learn to identify those who truly "feed" and energize us, he shows us how we can extend that same blessing to others.

—JIM DALY, president, Focus on the Family

John Townsend has done it again with a practical and urgent message for all of us who want the most from our relationships. Read this book and tap into an incredible source of renewable energy for your life.

—DRS. LES AND LESLIE PARROTT, authors, *Love Talk* and *Saving Your Marriage before It Starts*

In a world hyper-vigilant about nutrition for our bodies, this book is a breakthrough in challenging us to nourish something just as important: our relationships. Awesome neurological insights and biblical truths blended for true relational nourishment.

—DAVE BROWNE, former CEO, LensCrafters

Once I learned the principles found in *People Fuel*, I chose no longer to live a resource-deficient life. The relational nutrients you learn about in this book will elevate your relationships, leadership, and performance to new levels.

—MARK HOUSEHOLDER, president, Athletes in Action

Townsend gives a powerful prescription for people vitamins. Curious about the types of people you need to fuel your soul? This is the book for you!

—DRS. JOSH AND CHRISTI STRAUB, authors, *What Am I Feeling?*

Townsend offers a sanctuary for people at risk of drowning. The essential guide for understanding how to love and be loved by the people God has placed in our lives.

—JOSH KWAN, president, The Gathering

Townsend has the answers you need to find a healthy people balance. You'll feel your roots go deep into the soil of truth and your branches become vibrant and healthy.

—GREG LEITH, CEO, Convene

John Townsend's book tells it like it is: we need the right kind of people to fuel our lives well. I highly recommend *People Fuel*.

—PHIL ROBERTSON, founder, Duck Commander; star, *Duck Dynasty*

One of the most important books you can read if you want to master the art of knowing, serving, and loving people well—at work, at home, and in your sphere of influence.

—RAY HILBERT, cofounder, Truth at Work

PEOPLE
FUEL

PEOPLE FUEL

FILL YOUR TANK
for Life, Love, and Leadership

DR. JOHN TOWNSEND

 ZONDERVAN®

ZONDERVAN

People Fuel
Copyright © 2019 by John Townsend

Requests for information should be addressed to:
Zondervan, *3900 Sparks Dr. SE, Grand Rapids, Michigan 49546*

ISBN 978-0-310-34659-3 (hardcover)

ISBN 978-0-310-35408-6 (international trade paper edition)

ISBN 978-0-310-35409-3 (audio)

ISBN 978-0-310-34661-6 (ebook)

ISBN 978-1-404-11189-9 (special edition)

Published in association with Yates & Yates, www.yates2.com.

Cover design: Micah Kandros
Cover illustrations: supernick299/art-sonik/Shutterstock
Art direction: Curt Diepenhorst
Interior design: Kait Lamphere

Printed in the United States of America

19 20 21 22 23 24 25 26 27 28 /LSC/ 15 14 13 12 11 10 9 8 7 6 5 4 3 2 1

*To all those who believe that personal
and professional growth can be found
in the right kinds of relationships*

CONTENTS

THE PURPOSE OF THIS BOOK

I f you want life to work better for you, this book is for you. "Work better" covers a number of areas. It includes:

- ▶ More energy, positivity, and focus
- ▶ Higher-quality connections in family, friends, marriage, parenting, and dating
- ▶ More productivity and creativity in your leadership and work
- ▶ A growing spiritual, emotional, and personal life

The purpose of this book is to help you experience these benefits by providing you with the skills to get the most out of your relationships. The great majority of us are not tapping into the enormous power and energy that come from the right people.

We all know about the growth that comes from healthy nutrition, an exercise regimen, a positive attitude, being active, and a deep spiritual life. But few people know about the potential of relating to others in ways that transform us, give us energy, and help us succeed.

Many of us experience relationships as a drain or an obligation, something to do because others need us. We don't view them as something that builds us up as well. While we do have relationship responsibilities, such as parenting, marriage, or being a good friend, there is much more to the picture.

You will learn what is available for you in what are called the twenty-two relational nutrients. You'll see how to obtain them and use the energy they provide. And you'll learn who in your life to become closer to and who you may need more distance from.

It's my hope that you will improve not just your relationship life but your entire life, because that's how transforming the right people can be for you. This principle has worked for me and my clients for years, and this book is the culmination of the lessons and skills that have come from my efforts to help them.

PART 1

OUR RELATIONAL FOUNDATION

Everything significant starts with relationship. At the end of the day, your faith, your family, your work, and your leadership are all based on who you relate to and how you relate. Your life is motivated by love for others, being part of a family, a desire for intimacy and vulnerability, choosing to work on a great team, and creating a product or service that helps others. We are happiest when we know our lives revolve around people. Conversely, we are not ourselves, not our best selves, when we are isolated and alone.

Even more, think of how energized you are when you are around someone who gets you and encourages you. Your mind clears up, you are more positive, and you push through obstacles. It's like guzzling an energy drink and rebooting yourself.

Now think of the opposite experience: that person who drained you or, worse, was overly negative toward you. For me, the feeling after that encounter is that I'm walking through sludge, with very little mojo. So I have learned to embrace the first and, as much as possible, avoid the second.

But before we get to that, we need to understand and apply a foundational concept. If you'll commit to this first concept, good things will happen at so many levels.

CHAPTER 1

AN INDISPENSABLE TRUTH

I was working with a small group of leaders on a retreat. During the afternoon session, I asked a general question. "Okay, so you're a leader. What do you need most?"

It was silent for thirty seconds, and then the answers started coming. I began writing them on the whiteboard behind me.

"Alignment of vision."
"A great product."
"Innovation."
"Market penetration."
"Healthy culture."
"Resources."

When the answers died down, I said, "These are all great. But there's a missing ingredient—the most important ingredient, the one that will make all the difference. It will change everything, not only in your leadership but in your life." Then I wrote in larger letters:

You Need to Need

One attendee said, "We just told you what we needed, so why are you repeating yourself?"

I said, "Sorry to be confusing. I hope this will become clearer. There are two kinds of needs all humans have. The first is what I would call functional needs. Functional needs are the task requirements we all have to get things done. Most of the answers you gave on this board are functional needs. If we had been talking about your personal and family lives, we might have listed things like financial resources, food, shelter, good health, and a fulfilling career. This is the stuff that makes life work.

"But there is a second set of needs which are at least as important and are often neglected. They are our relational needs. Relational needs aren't about our tasks and our doing but are about what we receive from and supply to others. My experience of most people, whether it be in business or in the personal arena, is that they tend to do pretty well in getting their functional needs met but are deficient in getting their relational needs met. And unfortunately, these things we give and receive are indispensable. You cannot be all you need to be without them."

Another attendee spoke up. "Sounds a bit selfish to me, like 'me-ism'—it's all about my needs."

I said, "Sure, nobody should make life 'all about me,' and yes, that is selfish. But think about this for a second. How many of you listened to, supported, encouraged, or guided someone in the past seven days?"

Everyone raised their hands. "That's right," I said. "You guys do this all the time, because you care about the people in your lives and your organizations. And how many of you, in the last seven days, sat down and asked someone to provide for you the help that you provided for them?"

A couple of people raised their hands. "So why are most of you providing," I said, "that which you are not receiving?"

That question took us through the next two days at the retreat. It is also the premise of this book. The idea is simple: we need to need each other. People are the fuel for us to grow, be healthy, and prosper. God created a system in which we are to need not only him but also one another. That means we need to know what we need, recognize who can supply it, and have the skills to get it. And that will make a significant difference in life. More than significant—crucial. This is not an add-on or a luxury. The things we provide each other are a basic necessity. Let's get out of the thinking that goes like this: *Oh yes, asking others to support and help me. Great idea. I'll pencil that in for next month.* For this to work, it will need to be more frequent and more regular. You don't put off meals for a month, nor should you put off God's fuel.

And not only that, but to be the best person possible, you need the highest quality fuel possible. You want your car to have the highest-rated gasoline so it can perform at the highest level. You want to eat right and limit junk food. You want to experience inspiring books and videos and stay away from content that is a waste of time. So you also want to be around and learn from the best people available.

Let's begin with the idea of needs, because I think most of us have no idea of the benefits of having needs, and how life changes when we are engaged in our needs and the needs of others in the right way.

THE WHY OF NEED

What is a need? It is the requirement of a person or a machine or an organization for something essential. If the need is unmet, we experience trouble or damage. Without oxygen, we asphyxiate. Without food, we starve. And without shelter, we freeze or burn. People with strong constitutions can last without these for longer periods than others, but ultimately the need wins out and must be met.

God built a needs-meeting system into the universe as a critical aspect of how it runs. There are all sorts of needs.

1. In the marketplace, we transfer services and products we need to one another via the exchange of currency. We connect and have relationships built on commerce.

2. In the medical world, the systems in our body are interdependent. The heart needs the oxygen which the lungs supply. The lungs need blood for their survival. The brain needs the heart, and all the systems need the brain to tell them how to operate.

3. Artists and musicians need environments and relationships which are rich in experiences to create and express emotions and beauty. They are deeply moved by how they feel in their context and with the people in their lives.

4. Children are dependent on parents to protect, nurture, and develop them and are strongly tied to them emotionally.

The more we enter the world of need, whether functional or relational, the better life works.

The Bible is full of examples of how God interacts with us in the area of needs.

► At the creation, he provided food for people and animals (Gen. 1:29).

► IIe gave the people of Israel manna to sustain them on their journey through the wilderness (Ex. 16:31).

► Jesus said that those who hunger and thirst for righteousness will be filled (Matt. 5:6).

► Jesus fed the five thousand (John 6:1–12).

► Paul wrote that God will meet all our needs in Christ Jesus (Phil. 4:19).

► We are to receive mercy and grace in our time of need (Heb. 4:16).

► If we don't ask God for what we need, we won't have it (James 4:2).

I believe that the purpose behind this needs-meeting system is simple: God designed needs in order to foster relationship. When there is a lack on this side of the room and a provider for that lack on the other side, the two connect. They are now related. And that is a good thing. The one who lacks is made whole. The one who provides feels useful. And the two feel connected.

God didn't have to do it this way. He doesn't need the universe or us. He is self-sufficient. He desires and loves us, but we are not essential to him. He could have made it so that we were also self-sustaining little systems, spinning around in our lives without having to reach out for sustenance, support, resources, or love. But he didn't. He intertwined needs into the way things go.

God is, at his essence, about love: "We know and rely on the love God has for us. God is love. Whoever lives in love lives in God, and God in them" (1 John 4:16). And since love requires relationship, God is highly invested in relationships. He wants relationship with us, and he wants us to have relationships with each other.

Needs bring us together, into relationship. Think about the opposite situation, a person living in a self-sufficient and isolated manner, say, someone who lives away from others in the wilderness, surviving on his own without a supportive community, a loner who insists on not being dependent on anything or anyone. While we might admire his strength, we don't tend to make him a model for the whole and successful life.

At the same time, we have a loner part of ourselves as well, which has difficulty feeling and expressing our needs. I call it the sourcer-sourcee conflict.

SOURCER VERSUS SOURCEE

Recently, Austin, a friend of mine, called and asked to go to lunch. I wanted to meet with him, but my schedule was tight. So I said, "What's the agenda?" so I could determine whether it was an urgent matter. "Oh," he said, "just catching up. I wanted to see how you've been." It sounded casual, but I did want to see Austin, so I rearranged some meetings and we grabbed lunch.

To my surprise and dismay, he told me that his marriage with his wife, Heather, was in serious trouble and that he needed help in the worst way. The lunch quickly became an intense time of listening, finding out what the issues were, and coming up with a plan.

Fortunately, over time, things got better. We met again. I had identified some possible key issues and solutions and referred the couple to a great marital therapist. They stabilized and were on their way, though it took a lot of work. During a later coffee, when things had settled down, I asked Austin, "Do you remember our first meeting about your and Heather's conflict?"

"Sure I do," he said.

"I'm glad things worked out," I said, "but when I asked you what our agenda was, you said you wanted to catch up. Why didn't you tell me that you guys were in trouble?"

Austin looked embarrassed. "I didn't want you to think I was high maintenance."

"But you actually were high maintenance, right, at least at that time?"

"Yes, but I just hated thinking I was such a needy friend."

I thought about it a bit and asked, "So what if I had called you with a marriage problem and just flat out said I needed to meet with you quick because we were in trouble? Would you have thought of me as your high-maintenance, needy friend?"

"Of course not," he said. "We're friends, and that's what friends do—oh yeah . . ." And the lights came on for Austin. He realized that he was infinitely more comfortable meeting the needs of someone else than asking for his own to be met. He realized the disconnect in his thinking.

We all do this, to some extent. We feel much more comfortable in the role of sourcer than in the role of sourcee. The sourcer is the one providing for, helping, assisting, and supporting another—being the need meeter. The sourcee is the one who needs the help. Like Austin, we shy away from asking, while we are happy to give. Why is this? There are many obstacles to seeking help. Here are the predominant ones, and some suggestions for how to deal with them.

OBSTACLES TO ASKING

Feeling weak. For some people, saying, "I need something from you" doesn't make them feel strong and stable. Instead they feel weak, helpless, incomplete. My response: Weakness is a normal and good part of life. We all go through weak times, sometimes several times a day. There is nothing wrong with that, if the need is getting met and it's strengthening you to face the demands of reality. Feeling bad about weakness makes about as much sense as feeling bad about taking golf lessons because your swing is weak.

Feeling selfish. At times people feel that asking for something is making a self-centered move. They should be more giving, so they don't ask at all. My response: Certainly we aren't to be self-centered. But putting gas in your tank isn't selfish. It's a way to make yourself useful and productive.

Trust issues. Some people, unfortunately, have had painful relationships in which they learned that trusting and being vulnerable to someone important caused them hurt and rejection. Their response is to either isolate from others or become a consummate giver, because that prevents them from ever having to be vulnerable again. My response: Don't let the actions of one hurtful person keep you from all the great relationships God has for you. You will need to work through the hurt and stop projecting that person's qualities onto humanity in general. My book *Beyond Boundaries* is a resource that can help you rebuild trust.

Shame. Shame is the feeling that a part of us is so defective that we cannot be accepted or loved. It is that mistake, attitude, behavior, failure, or difficult season in the past that we judge ourselves for. We are convinced that if others knew about it, they would judge or leave us. It is a very painful feeling and can keep us from expressing our needs. My response: Find a few proven and safe people and slowly let them know this part of you. You will be amazed at the grace and relief you will feel from their warmth and acceptance.

Not feeling deserving. Some people refrain from asking because they think they are not deserving of or have not earned the privilege of asking. My response: How would you feel if a close friend told you that they avoided asking you for help because they didn't deserve it? You would probably feel sad that an opportunity was missed. The reality is that we were not designed to work to deserve love, support, a listening ear, or help. That is a transactional viewpoint of relationships, and it will destroy them. Life is not about being nice to people who have earned our love by mowing our lawn and washing our car. It's about loving those around us because they have needs. So change the equation: "No, I don't deserve support and help. But I need it. And that's enough."

Concern about burdening others. As in Austin's situation, people refrain from asking because they don't want others to expend a great amount of time and effort on their behalf. My response: Certainly we shouldn't demand that others give up too much for us. But that is a case of fragilizing others. We fragilize by not taking into account that other people are resilient and strong and can determine their own boundaries and how they choose to spend their time and energy. Let them decide for themselves; it's a sign that you respect them.

Confusing the functional and the relational. Sometimes we do ask and do provide, but we are out of balance. We lean toward the functional side—favors, errands, advice, and wisdom—when sometimes we just need to make a connection with another safe human and that's enough. In so many relationships, learning to be emotionally present is often the solution. But we tend to go overboard on advice and guidance, most of the time because we don't have the right skills, feel anxious, and are trying to do something helpful. This book will provide you with the right balance, helping you determine when advice is the way to go and when there are other solutions.

"I need," in the relational realm, tends to be a cringeworthy statement, and "need" a cringey word in particular. It's acceptable to say, "I need some advice on finances" or "I need some parenting tips," as these statements are more functional. But it's not as easy to say, "I need to get lunch with you because life is challenging and I just need to talk." We feel weak or ashamed, as though something were wrong with us.

There is a funny YouTube video called "It's Not About the Nail" which makes this point. It is a scenario involving a couple in which the woman just wants to be heard and understood and the man wants to solve the problem. It illustrates how far apart we are sometimes in this area.

This may get worse. Some people are concerned that if they uncork a few needs, there may be a flood of other and deeper needs, and it's just better not to go there in the first place. My response: Yes, it can get worse, especially if you have a long-term pattern of not asking for needs to be met. So take it slowly and gradually. Just ask for a few things. If you find your emotions becoming intense and painful, see a competent therapist. They have studied this and know the answers and the process.

Access problems. Some people don't ask because they simply experience very few needs. They rarely, if ever, feel a need for being accepted or comforted or helped. They are even sometimes puzzled by all the needs of people around them. My response: There are people who have had so many healthy experiences of being loved, helped, and accepted that their own need states are not as frequent or intense. But for the majority of people, those who don't feel these needs do have them, but they can't experience them. They don't have emotional access to their needs. This falls into the category of attachment issues. If this is your situation, this book will help a great deal, as the more we practice dealing with needs, the more we will be able to feel what is there inside.

The leader's dilemma. Leaders especially hesitate to ask for their needs and prefer to be on the giving end. This is understandable because they want to be good models for success and maturity and instill confidence in their people that the organization is being led well. My response: I work with some extremely successful and high-performing leaders. And the solution is that while they certainly want to keep colleagues' confidence in them high, they privately have relationships, away from the boardroom, in which they let down their hair and get their needs met.

Misunderstanding of the Bible. Many people neglect to bring their needs to others, because they feel that they should ask only God to supply their needs. They believe that to ask others means that they don't trust God. My response to this is a story, followed by a Bible lesson, then application.

Before I attended grad school to earn a degree in psychology, I attended Dallas Theological Seminary to learn the Bible. One of my mentors was Dr. Howard Hendricks, who taught me a great deal about life and leadership. His kindness, interest, and wisdom were a great help to me in my formative years.

I was in chapel one morning, and Dr. Hendricks was speaking. During his talk, he made the point, "When you graduate from here and go into your ministry or career, it's a good idea that you not have a best friend."

I was a bit confused by that statement, as I had several close friends and I thought they made my life better. Dr. Hendricks said that we should put all our trust in God and that best friends could lead us astray and even get in the way of living a life of faith. I remember thinking, *Well, if Moses said it, it's just true.* I really did look up to him!

A couple of years later, after I graduated, a seminary friend and I were talking and he said, "Did you hear about Dr. Hendricks' chapel message a few weeks ago?" I said no, and he said, "It was really interesting. He said, 'You may have heard me speak here a couple of years ago and say that it wasn't a good idea to have a best friend. I was wrong. You'd better have a best friend.'"

Now I was really confused. It's not often that one of your personal rock stars does a one-eighty in his teaching. As it happened, though, by this time I was in the habit of having coffee with Dr. Hendricks when I was in Dallas visiting friends. So at our next meeting, I asked him, "Tell me about your recanting what you said in chapel about best friends." And he told me the story.

The seminary had a policy of helping graduates who had a major struggle after they left the school. This could involve burnout, a church split, a moral failure, or a serious depression. Pastors are under enormous pressure, 24/7. And the way the seminary helped them was to have Dr. Hendricks meet with them to understand their situations and help them heal and rebuild their lives.

He found out that during these times, the great majority of the struggling graduates had one thing in common: they had no close friends. They were without deep, safe confidants with whom they could say anything and receive support and acceptance.

So Dr. Hendricks went back to his Bible and researched the issue. And that was how he concluded that God designed us for deep and trusting relationships. Dr. Hendricks saw that best friends were necessary for a healthy life. Being the person of character that he was, he had no trouble saying, "I was wrong" in public. He was interested only in what was true and real.

Around this time, I was working on my doctorate in psychology and was studying the human condition. I too began looking at what the Bible says about these matters. And I was amazed at how many passages talk about how people are meant to supply each other's needs. Here are a few of the ones that spoke to me.

- *Genesis 2:18.* "It is not good for the man to be alone." This is not a verse about marriage. It is about relationship, the fact that in a perfect universe, where there was perfect connection with God, there was a "not good" situation, because Adam had no other human being to connect with.
- *Ecclesiastes 4:9–10.* "Two are better than one, because they have a good return for their labor: if either of them falls down, one can help the other up. But pity anyone who falls and has no one to help them up." This passage is not about God meeting our need; it's about a person doing it.
- *Matthew 26:38.* "Then [Jesus] said to them, "My soul is overwhelmed with sorrow to the point of death. Stay here and keep watch with me." Jesus asks Peter, James, and John to be with him while he is in prayer to God, in deep torment. This is a picture of even Jesus asking for support from people.

▶ *2 Corinthians 7:6.* "God, who comforts the downcast, comforted us by the coming of Titus." During Paul's trials, God could have comforted him with an angel, a Bible passage, visitation by the Holy Spirit, or a miracle, all of which God does. But in this instance, he sent a person.

▶ *1 Peter 4:10.* "Each of you should use whatever gift you have received to serve others, as faithful stewards of God's grace in its various forms." This passage says that people are the delivery system of God's grace.

This all means that God meets our needs from two directions: "vertically," through prayer, the Bible, the Holy Spirit, the spiritual disciplines, and surrender; and "horizontally," through people. We need both sources. In some way we do not fully understand, God set up a system in which he alone (the vertical) is not enough. That system without the horizontal is, according to the Bible, "not good" (Gen. 2:18). Henry Cloud and I write about this in our book *How People Grow.*

So when I mention a misunderstanding of the Bible as another reason we don't ask others to meet our needs, you can see it's a big deal. We have to get our theological hats on straight and realize that God uses people, all the time, to help us survive, grow, heal, and succeed.

"GOD, MY SPOUSE, AND MAX" SYNDROME

Sometimes an individual will be partly beyond just vertically bonded. They do get some nutrients besides prayer and the Bible, but it's still pretty limited. I call it the "God, my spouse, and Max" syndrome. During a break at one of my seminars, I was talking with a businessman about our need for others. He said, "I really understand this concept you're talking about. We need more than prayer and Bible study. And I don't go it alone in my life. I do get my needs met. I have God, my wife, and my dog Max. God provides his love and guidance. My wife knows all my fears and failures and listens to me. Max accepts me no matter what. So I'm set."

I said, "Yes, there are a lot of positives to getting your needs met by these three supportive sources. It's also a positive for you that there is at least one human being in the mix. A supportive and loving marriage is a great thing. But if the only human you are truly vulnerable with is your wife, you are in relational deficit."

He was a bit puzzled. "She's really all I need. We trust each other implicitly and share everything. I have lots of friends, but she is the one I share my deepest concerns and fears with."

"That is great, and congratulations on having a deep and solid marriage. But what if you don't know what you don't know?"

"Go on."

"What if there are available to you more sources for acceptance, support, wisdom, and encouragement than your wife? Is it possible that because you don't experience a need for more, you assume that you don't need more? The Bible says much more about how we are all to relate to each other in general than it does about marriage. Just search in your Bible app for 'one another,' and see the many passages that regard how we are to treat each other and meet each other's needs. That doesn't take anything away from marriage; it's one of God's greatest gifts. It does mean, however, that we are designed to engage in healthy, deep, and meaningful relationships in addition to our marriages."

Whenever I mention the "God, my spouse, and Max" syndrome to an audience of couples, several wives will come up to me afterward and say, "I love him and we are very close, but I do get a bit burned out on being the only person he can be open with. I wish he had other guys to really relate to." (Lately, a number of husbands have made a similar comment about their wives.)

And that is one of the reasons I wrote this book, to provide a clear and practical way to experience much more of what God has for us all. I was doing a life evaluation of a coaching client and identified him as having the syndrome: close to God, great marriage, and a great dog (not named Max). One of my conclusions was that he was in relational deficit.

"What does that mean?" he asked.

"It's similar to having an iron deficit or a calcium deficit in your bloodstream," I said. "You may not be aware of the impact of the deficit, but it's there somewhere."

He didn't like getting the news, because it meant doing some work finding and implementing the right sorts of relationships, and he was a busy person. But he wanted to receive all that God had for him and realize his full potential. He entered the process I will describe in this book. Within a few months, he told me, "I had no idea that things could be better in so many areas of my life. My joy, energy, creativity, career, family relationships, and even my marriage, are all better."

Sometimes we don't know what we don't know.

So we are fuel for each other, great and necessary fuel. And our fueling comes through relationship, specifically through "relational nutrients," a term I will describe in the book.

THE GENDER DIFFERENCE

I mentioned earlier that more women tell me their husbands need to branch out relationally than the converse. I think it's just true that women have an edge on men in being wired for relationship, and men are more wired for activity. But it's just an edge; we're not talking about two different universes. I don't believe in gender theories that state how totally different men and women are. The reality is that we are more alike than we are different. The genders have much more in common with each other than we have distinctions. We all are created in God's image. We all need to be attached deeply. We all need to have our own identities and boundaries. We all need to accept our flaws and those of others. We all need to find our purpose in life and express our talents to accomplish that purpose. Women and men share all of this, and this encompasses the majority of life. If we put the genders in two circles on a Venn diagram, most of the space would be intersected space, and the minority of the space would be solely male and solely female.

The implications are that both genders need to work on this. Most men have to work harder on this than most women do. But all of us need to make sure we are getting our needs met, and providing those needs to others, in the best way.

OUT OF BALANCE

It is just as true that our relational needs are no less critical than our functional needs. Longitudinal studies have proven over and over that without significant supportive relationships, we have more psychological dysfunctions, we have more health problems, and we die sooner.[1]

As I mentioned in the story of the retreat, most of us are much more comfortable talking about our functional needs than our relational needs. You can make statements like "I need a job in which I can express my passions and skills" or "I need to lose weight" or "I need a break today" without angst or shame. There is no worry someone might think less of us.

When we move from the functional realm into the relational realm, we tend to be pretty comfortable as long as it's the other person's need. There is little insecurity in saying, "I'm meeting with Samantha for lunch; she needs to talk about some issues with her and her mom." We are glad to help with that person's need. Most of us feel compassion and want to provide in some way.

But when the relational need is our own, the conflict arises. It's harder to be Samantha or Sam, the one calling for support. We shy away from feeling that way or expressing ourselves like that. But we need to push past this and learn that asking doesn't diminish us. It provides others an opportunity to express their support for us. And that in turn brings them toward us and improves both parties.

So in summary, to set up what we'll cover in the rest of the book:

▶ God created a need-meeting system that is part of how the universe works.
▶ The things we need are indispensable to life working right, and not a luxury.
▶ We were designed to get needs met and provide for others' needs.
▶ God meets our needs vertically (directly) and horizontally (through people).
▶ Needs can be functional or relational.
▶ Our relational needs are a significant predictor of emotional, relational, and medical health as well as success.
▶ We tend to be more comfortable meeting others' needs than asking for our own.
▶ We tend to be more comfortable in the functional (advice and help) arena than in the relational arena.

From this point, we need to look at how this works in our personal growth. In the next chapter, you'll see a simple model of how relationships are key in becoming a mature and complete person.

CHAPTER 2

THE PATH-TO-GROWTH TREE

"O ne of my stretch goals for this year is to lose sixty pounds."

Allison, an owner of a small financial services business, made that announcement to her team on the first day with our leadership coaching program. It was a serious moment, for both Allison and the team. During our briefing meetings before the program's launch, Allison had mentioned a long-term struggle with weight and how discouraged about it she was. So when she committed to an actual number and elevated the priority to one of the three stretch goals that members have for a given year, she was expressing a great deal of vulnerability and courage to the team. The group, in its turn, was moved by how open she was about her frustrations over previous attempts and committed to Allison to be there for her any way they could.

As I got to know Allison, I was struck by everything she had already been doing right about weight loss for years. Highly intelligent and inquisitive, she had researched body metabolism, nutrition, even brain chemistry. She had also created structures such as calendaring gym times, getting a trainer, and using the leadership team as an accountability system. And yet she had no pattern of success. She was stuck on the yo-yo cycle.

At the same time, I began noticing a pattern with Allison in our group. More than anyone else, she was the giver. She provided great financial solutions for team members who had money challenges, as she was highly proficient in that world. Not only that, but she was a relational giver as well. When someone was discouraged, stressed, or beating themselves up for some failure, Allison was warm and empathic and had the right encouraging things to say. She had an intuitive ability to feel what others were experiencing and go to the heart of the matter. And beyond that, between our monthly meetings, she was the one who reached out most often and most consistently to the team members via face-to-face contact, phone calls, and texts.

But there was another side of Allison's engagement with her group. She never asked for anything relational. Her conversations were almost all about either the needs of the team or some functional need, such as how to parent her teen better or how to align her employees with the company's vision. It was never about asking for support or just for someone to listen.

Though everyone appreciated how helpful she was, I and the other members began observing the dissonance with Allison. In our group sessions, one of them might say, "So how are you doing?" And she would adroitly divert the focus away from herself and onto others, saying things like, "I'm doing fine, but I've been concerned about you, Travis. It seems like what's going on in your company and with your kids is a lot to bear, and it feels like it must be overwhelming."

Fortunately, several members of the team were pretty mature in the emotional-relational arena and wouldn't let the diversion slide forever. They were concerned about her. One of them finally said, "Allison, I have to be honest with you. I don't feel as close in our relationship as I'd like to. I sort of know you, but I don't think I really know you, at least not like I do the rest of the team."

Allison was a bit hurt by this. She said, "I'm sorry, but I really don't understand. I think I'm all in for you guys. I really am committed to you. You mean a lot to me, and this is a surprise."

I took over at that point and asked the team, "Well, let's get a baseline. Does anyone else have this experience of Allison?"

Most of the members spoke up and said something similar.

Now Allison was just plain confused. "What am I doing wrong?"

I said, "First of all, you're doing a *lot* right, so let's not lose sight of that. But I agree with the team that you shy away from being vulnerable with us and bringing your real needs to the team. I rarely hear you ask for support, listening, acceptance, or anything like that. And the problem is that people don't really know us until they know our vulnerabilities and needs. I think the team knows your care, your support, and your encouragement. But it tends to end there.

"I'd like for you to think about why it is that you don't ask from this group what you provide to them. More to the point, I'd like for you to talk with us about what the feeling and experience would be if you did ask for support in some way."

Allison was quiet and reflective. Then she said, "I think I'm just happier when I take care of people."

I said, "Sure, that's a good thing. But your team members are happy when you give to them as well, and you don't have that kind of happiness. Keep exploring what you think the experience would be. I think it has some negative connotations."

Allison said, "I think it would be a very negative experience if I asked."

"Why?"

"Because if you guys had any sense, you would pull away from me. You don't need one more needy, high-maintenance person in your lives."

The group was surprised and saddened to hear Allison speak of herself with such harsh words.

I said, "That's a pretty tough self-assessment, Allison. Is that how you experience the team's needs?"

She began to protest. "No, not at all. I love you guys! I am so comfortable with the challenges you have, and I would never see you in a negative light!"

I knew I didn't have to say anything more, because I saw the wheels turning in her head.

Her face reddened and she said, "So you're wondering why the disconnect here?"

"I am."

That led us into a great deal of productive but difficult team discovery with Allison about why she was so judging of her own needs but so gracious with those of others. She had grown up in a home where her parents needed her to be highly responsible and caring, above and beyond what a child should have to be. She was the one who, at eleven years old, would calm her mom down when she was upset. When her teenage brother, who was into drugs and acting out, had episodes, she made sure her dad was not too upset. The technical term for this issue is the parentified child. The child had to parent the parents. Allison was eleven years old on the outside and thirty years old on the inside.

One thing parentified children never do is ask for their needs to be met. The unspoken covenant in Allison's family was that she was to be the sourcer and not the sourcee. The fear was that if she had a problem, was overwhelmed, or failed, it would bring the whole family down, as she was always the strong one, at least in her mind.

The lights quickly came on for Allison as she began to understand all this. She had no room in her head for her own needs. She perceived herself as a sourcer, a helper and supporter of others, a strong person without needs.

As Allison processed all this with the group, they began validating her needs, acknowledging how right and proper it was that she ask for what she did not have. They would say, "I'd honestly feel closer to you if you said you'd like to talk about yourself and what your struggles are" and "Now that I know a bit about your history, I feel a great deal of compassion for what it was like to have to be the glue for everyone in your home." The group began to support her, reach out to her, and express compassion for her, doing what the body of Christ is supposed to do with each other: "comfort those in any trouble with the comfort we ourselves receive from God" (2 Cor. 1:4). They did this from time to time, during the course of several days' meetings.

At first Allison pushed back, saying things like, "Guys, I'm fine. Other people here have bigger challenges than I do" and "Can we get the spotlight off me?"

Then an amazing thing happened. During one session, Allison began to express what it had felt like to have to be the strong one, with no room for needs, and how hard that was. She had been getting it cognitively, but now it was happening emotionally. And she started having feelings of loneliness, sadness, and being overwhelmed and beyond herself. The group had been pouring relational nutrients into her and challenging her beliefs about herself, and she began feeling safe enough to acknowledge what was true.

This changed everything for Allison. She became more open and vulnerable about her career, her marriage, her parenting, and her childhood. She brought up struggles and asked for support. In a sense, she truly joined the team, because she now related to them as they were relating to her and each other.

And she began losing weight. Gradually and consistently, the pounds began dropping off. Allison had the aha experience of realizing that the only place she could go for her needs was to food, rather than relationship. Food had always been the comfort and support for stress and struggle, and it protected her from having to take relational risks. But as she became more comfortable asking for her needs, the food was much less necessary.

With all the weight loss structures and strategies she already had in her life, the missing piece was what is technically called "internalizing the good" from others. It has been several years since Allison went through the program, and she is still maintaining a healthy weight and lifestyle.

I have never worked with what I would consider a balanced, growing, and healthy person—leader, parent, spouse, or any other category—who has not found substantial benefit in the elements of Allison's story. The elements are:

- ▸ A struggle or challenge in some life area
- ▸ Attempts to solve it that don't finish the job
- ▸ An unawareness that underlying relational needs are important
- ▸ Shame and resistance to identifying and expressing the needs

- ▸ Support and grace from others, affirming that it's normal and okay
- ▸ Taking in the nutrients from relationship
- ▸ Improvement in the challenge area

This is simply the pattern, the way God's process of growth seems to work most often. I want to offer a simple model for this.

It's based on a story Jesus taught. "Then he told this parable: 'A man had a fig tree growing in his vineyard, and he went to look for fruit on it but did not find any. So he said to the man who took care of the vineyard, "For three years now I've been coming to look for fruit on this fig tree and haven't found any. Cut it down! Why should it use up the soil?" "Sir," the man replied, "leave it alone for one more year, and I'll dig around it and fertilize it. If it bears fruit next year, fine! If not, then cut it down""" (Luke 13:6–9).

The story was told in the context of the nation of Israel's fruit-lessness in following God in heart and mind. Jesus was illustrating that while God requires fruit, at the same time he patiently allows for some digging in the soil to enrich the plant, hopefully helping it to become fruitful.

The same thing is true in our personal, spiritual, career, relational, and emotional worlds. We all want good fruit in our lives but often, like Allison, find ourselves frustrated with the outcome. We may have tried what we think is everything yet still find ourselves without the results we want. So let's start where the parable starts and understand how God's process works. The figure on page 37 will help you visualize the structure.

While this is not a precisely linear model of how human growth works, it helps to show how good, desirable fruit gets produced.

Let's move on to the fruit.

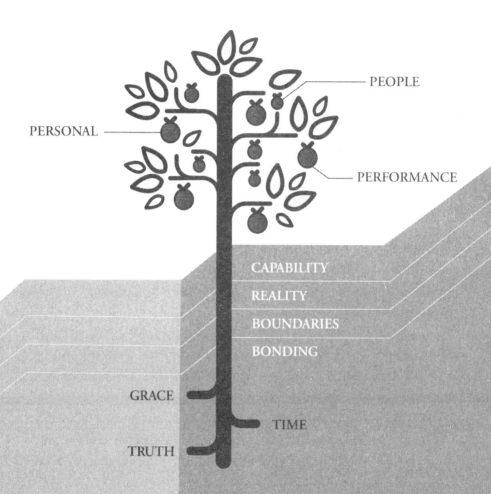

CHAPTER 3

THE FRUIT

There are three fruit categories by which all of us measure our lives, happiness, and success. I call them the three Ps.

1. PERSONAL

Personal refers to anything in our lives that falls within our purview as individuals. When we talk about a personal problem or a personal challenge, that is the arena we are in. There are several types of personal fruit that matter to us.

1. *Behavior.* Our behavior is simply our actions, the things we do. Good behavior fruit refers to a life in which we are in control of our choices and don't have areas in which we are out of control. We don't struggle with major bad habits (eating problems, too much time online) or addictions (alcohol, drugs, sexual), which would be undesirable fruit, and we lead an active, free, disciplined, and productive life.

2. *Thoughts.* Our brains think all the time. The research indicates that our brains are even working while we are asleep. We consider who God is, and we ponder what's for lunch. We plan for our next step in our careers, and we think about the news we are reading. We are thinking beings. A mind that is operating in a reality-based and healthy way is good fruit:

"We take captive every thought to make it obedient to Christ" (2 Cor. 10:5). But when our thoughts are not life affirming and healthy, that is not the fruit you want. Have you ever had an obsessional dark thought in your mind that would not leave, no matter what you did to get rid of it? Troublesome thoughts can divert energy from the right life.

3. *Values.* Probably the most personal of the personal fruits, values are those fundamental stances we take on what is most important in life. They help shape our direction and choices. A value of being a growing and improving person will help your life to become fulfilling, while a value of putting yourself first all the time will not lead to a great life. In the world of leadership, a value of expressing your talents to run a great business is a good-fruit value. A value that says, "People owe me a good life and success" is not a helpful one.

4. *Emotions.* We are emotional creatures. We have various passions and feelings throughout each day. A life of good-fruit emotions has two characteristics. First, there is context appropriateness, meaning that our feelings make sense in our situation. If a driver on the freeway flips you off and you are so angry that it ruins your next hour, your anger isn't context appropriate. Maybe thirty seconds would be healthier. Second, there is access to emotions, meaning that you can feel your feelings, both positive and negative. They are accessible to you. Some people are great thinkers but struggle to experience and express their feelings, or most of their feelings. Something has walled them off from feeling what is really there, and this can cause them to make poor decisions in their relationships and in their career.

2. PEOPLE

The second P is about the relationships in our life, both personal and professional.

The people we are engaged with in life matter a great deal to us:

▸ Our spouse or the person we are dating
▸ Friends
▸ Kids
▸ Family members
▸ Coworkers
▸ Church family
▸ Neighbors

Relationships like these can be agony or ecstasy. They can help life be meaningful, rich, and growth producing. And the hard ones can take up way too much of our bandwidth. One of the most common reasons people go to see a counselor is because there are difficulties with a relationship.

In my line of work as a consultant to leaders and their organizations, I have seen a great number of people issues. One thing I have observed is that no matter how great your product, service, strategy, and systems, the right people can accelerate everything, and the wrong people can take you down.

A business owner I was working with underwent a tech-based disruption of his industry. Tech advances had quickly made a large part of his company obsolete. He had to spend two years retooling his business, overhauling everything about it. This was an incredibly stressful time for him. He had to downsize everything, and he had a very difficult cash position.

However, he had assembled the right kinds of friends and the right kinds of key employees. He leaned on them, teamed with them, and persevered with them. Ultimately, he righted the ship and things went well. As we were talking about this and I complimented his success, he said, "There was a lot of hard work and some good ideas. But I never could have done this without the help of the people who stayed with me and supported me."

Often we evaluate our lives and others' lives by the quality of relationships. Think about all the times you heard of someone who is successful in business but whose relationship life has been a series of train wrecks. We don't tend to think of these individuals as role models.

There are two qualities of people fruit that tend to matter most and make the most difference in our relationships.

1. Vulnerability

Vulnerability is the act of taking risks to express negative parts of ourselves in our relationships. It is "taking off the fig leaf" and letting someone see and know us, naked and unashamed. The negative parts can include many aspects of our lives and experiences.

- ▶ Mistakes we have made
- ▶ Struggles that we have
- ▶ Weaknesses we have not resolved
- ▶ Sins we deal with
- ▶ Needs that have not been met
- ▶ Emotions that are hard to discuss

Individuals who have healthy people fruit have several friends with whom they are in regular contact, who both give and receive vulnerability. The capacity to be vulnerable allows us to truly know each other, to support each other, and to be a source of life and energy for each other. People who do not have several vulnerable relationships often struggle with isolation, energy problems, and self-doubt.

Jesus himself was vulnerable. On the cross, he didn't pretend to be strong and invulnerable, but instead, in his agony, he asked his Father, "Why have you forsaken me?" (Matt. 27:46). That sort of honesty in our relationships is a hallmark of great health.

I was working with the team of a successful private equity company who tended to be a bit guarded with one another, keeping a stiff upper lip. The company had turned to me because people were operating in silos and not collaborating well. I conducted a training with them on professional vulnerability, its benefits and how it works.

During the debriefing I did with the partners about how the training had gone, one of the partners looked at the person sitting next to him and said, "I haven't been vulnerable with you about how insecure I feel with you sometimes, and that's why I avoid you."

The other person was surprised to hear this. "Wait a minute. I feel insecure around you!"

We entered into a deeper conversation, and the result was that the two began to trust and engage with each other in a much healthier and more productive way.

Unfortunately, in our culture vulnerable relationships don't happen as often as they should. People feel they have to have it together, be totally positive, and not show weaknesses. They are surrounded by warm bodies, but there is no deep connection. The one word that best describes the situation is *empty*. On the other hand, a few vulnerable relationships will always create a sense of connectedness.

2. The Capacity to Solve Relational Problems

The second critical aspect of great people fruit is the ability for our relationships to be so safe and honest that we can solve relational problems together. I'm not referring to having friends help us with parenting issues or business challenges. I mean problems within the relationship itself.

With any significant connection with someone, over time we will disagree, bug each other, hurt each other's feelings, or separate from one another. No relationship of any gravitas is without its speed bumps. It's just the nature of being human. If you have never disagreed with someone important in your life, one of you is not necessary.

But the great relationships are those which employ the love, persistence, character, and skills required to work things out and move on. The connections are often stronger once the storm has been weathered.

This capacity to solve problems is a rare commodity today. How often have you expressed a difference of opinion or experienced a conflict, and after that the relationship was never the same or even ended?

I was hired by a large home furnishings company to fix the relationship between two top executives, a woman and a man, in the marketing department. Things had gotten so bad between them that by this point they were no longer speaking.

I had a two-hour conversation with them to help matters. It was a lot of work for all three of us. Basically, the woman was easily triggered by any sort of criticism, even when spoken as kindly as possible, and the man unfortunately never criticized kindly. So it was a match not made in heaven.

I was handling statements like, "You are the most disorganized person I know. How can you keep your job?" and "You are not only critical; you are judgmental. I don't have to listen to this from you," followed by leaving the room.

Eventually it all got sorted out in a positive way, and they worked out their relationship issues well. But imagine the impact on the company before that. Executives were telling me that it was affecting, and infecting, the whole organization. Performance was down, culture was in the tank, and just getting things done was derailed.

The same is true in our personal lives. When you care about someone, you want to be able to disagree, argue in healthy ways, solve problems, make decisions, and get back to love and connection. When that can't happen, we feel disconnected, alone, frustrated, and sad.

This is why the problem-solving aspect of people fruit is so important, and why I have written so many *Boundaries* books on healthy ways to deal with this. The Bible teaches how important it is to be able to solve problems with each other through the right conversations: "Brothers and sisters, if someone is caught in a sin, you who live by the Spirit should restore that person gently. But watch yourselves, or you also may be tempted" (Gal. 6:1).

Being able to have vulnerable and honest relationships is simply a great way to go through life, personally and professionally.

3. PERFORMANCE

This third fruit is about the task, or doing, aspect of life. We spend a tremendous amount of time in performance. Most of that time is spent in the workplace, where we need to perform at certain levels in order to meet goals and deadlines.

A life of good performance fruit is one in which we are productive and successful in the working realm. Here are some examples.

> ▶ *Mission.* A CEO who feels that one of her main purposes in life is to lead her IT business in such a way that she knows people all over the world benefit from its products and services
> ▶ *Career.* A website designer who loves his work, is highly capable, and is sought out for projects
> ▶ *Finance.* A couple in the Midwest who, though they have a medium-range income, are frugal and money smart and not only end up with a healthy retirement but also generously give to charities and missions they support
> ▶ *Service.* A single mom who is gifted at helping support and serve families of prison inmates and in her off hours spends time talking with them and helping them with meals, getting clothes for their kids, and finding community

People who have good performance fruit tend to feel engaged, satisfied, productive, and energized. They talk about it with their family and friends and stay interested.

But when the fruit is not so healthy, it's a different scenario.

> ▶ *Mission.* A man spends years fruitlessly searching for his purpose on earth. He has talents but can't find his place. He doesn't feel useful or focused. His frustration is that he knows he has significant potential to make a difference, but for some reason it hasn't occurred, and he is baffled.

- *Career.* A woman shuffles from company to company, in different industries and sectors. She has had several starts at a career but for some reason can't stay with any of them. So she has a *Groundhog Day* experience, in which she is constantly beginning but never deepening and building on her career life.
- *Finance.* A man in real estate makes a good income but can't save for the future. He gets stuck, not in the high cost of living but in the cost of high living. His wife is disappointed and anxious.
- *Service.* A woman feels deeply about the plight of children exploited in sex trafficking. She empathizes with them and reads extensively about the situation. She attends church meetings on the topic. Yet she can't make progress on some sort of action plan in which she can get engaged and do something helpful. She doesn't know if she should become committed enough to join an organization or start her own ministry or simply help out in a natural and organic way when she finds opportunity.

What a contrast, and what a difficult way to go through life. Our performance is a critical aspect of the fruit we experience and need.

Let's take a look at the big picture of our life's fruit. If you have productive habits, positive thoughts, the right core values, and healthy emotional expression in important relationships in which you can be vulnerable, be yourself, and disagree and solve problems, those are all good indicators of a healthy, happy life. Not a perfect one but one anyone would want. And that is the vision for where life should go.

But if you had a life in which you were constantly sidetracked by bad habits (even to the point of addiction), were plagued by negative or obsessive thoughts, weren't sure about what is important in life, and were suffering emotionally? That is a nightmare experience and certainly one to avoid.

THE LEVELS MATTER

You don't have to have awful, depressing fruit to need to take some actions about it. The sooner we pay attention to small problems, the less likely they are to become large ones. A negative month in sales should warn us to do something so that there is not a negative year. And a day when you and your spouse aren't speaking should be addressed so that it doesn't become a week.

I train the coaches in my organization to help their clients figure out, during the early stages of their relationship with them, what to work on, by using a simple table I developed.

Area	Struggling to Good	Good to Great	Great to Optimal
Income			
Expenses			
Leadership			
Culture			
Strategy			
Marketing			
Sales			
Operations			
Administration			

The area column can have any number of categories of concern. But each category must have a commitment check on it. Either things are struggling and the client wants them to be resolved (struggling to good), they are okay but need to be improved (good to great), or they are great and the client would like to see them going as well as possible (great to optimal).

I use this chart because it's sometimes hard for a client to look at negative information about their work or organization. It takes a certain amount of openness and a lack of defensiveness to have a coach, and it can be a bit embarrassing to discuss one's challenges. Leaders are often enculturated to think so positively that they can't identify the problems they are facing. That's why the great-to-optimal column exists. Hypothetically, if someone hires a coach and insists that every area of work is going great, there is still somewhere to improve on things.

Look at this as basically a checklist of fruit. Your personal life, people life, and performance life may all be working well. But I promise you, not every area is optimized. There is somewhere to make things better.

So we all are somewhere between the scenarios of seriously negative fruit and optimal fruit. And since we want to continue moving toward growth, we want to take steps in that direction. But let's look at one of the passes we tend to take, and why that is doomed to fail us.

YELLING AT THE FRUIT

I was meeting with Dylan, the senior vice president of sales for an IT company I was working with. He was a talented and energetic guy, but the sales department was struggling. Dylan was concerned, as the responsibility for its performance was on his shoulders.

I asked him why he thought things were down.

He said, "Honestly, I think I'm the problem. I can't blame the company or my people. I just have not been spending the time with my directs that I should be. If I worked with them more in resourcing, clarifying their roles, and supporting them, I think we'd be in different shape."

"Glad you are looking at yourself first, and let's suppose that's the case," I said. "So why do you think you aren't spending enough time with your folks?"

"Probably because I take too much time with my own clients," he said. "I like them, and I like selling anyway, so I default in that direction."

"Makes sense. How do you want to change that ratio of time?"

Dylan thought a moment. "I just need to do it from now on. I'll just start doing it."

Having worked with the company and Dylan for a while, I said, "You sure that's all? With all due respect, I've been with you when you've made commitments like this before, and generally they don't last very long." I was referring to times when he would make strong commitments to change several issues, such as timeliness, getting reports in, and the like. None of these were serious enough to jeopardize his job, because he usually had stellar results. But the pattern was there.

"This is different," he said, looking directly at me with a serious expression. "I've been flaky with my directs, it's not good for anyone, and I just need to do it better."

I hoped for the best, but unfortunately Dylan's good intentions didn't pan out, and sixty days later we were having another conversation. This time, however, it was more critical, with his job on the line.

We'll circle back to Dylan in a minute, and there was a better resolution to this. But this story is an example of something common to human nature, something that I call yelling at the fruit. When we aren't happy with something in the three Ps, we tend to concentrate on changing the outcome, forgetting that hardly anything happens in a vacuum. There is always a source underlying a problem. Dylan was uberfocused on simply changing his priorities, and that is how he handled most of his business challenges.

Barbi and I have a small apple tree on our property. We like having apples to eat, straight from the back yard. Suppose I woke up one morning wanting apple slices to put on my cereal. So I go out and discover that instead of large, juicy apples, the tree has these wimpy, small fruits hanging from it.

I could say in my frustration to the tree, "You and your apples suck! I need really good ones, not these losers! Get your act together and get me some great fruit!"

If the apple tree could talk, it would probably say, "I'm not the problem here. I'm happy to make great apples. But you haven't been watering me or aerating the soil or putting the right amount of calcium, nitrates, and phosphates into the ground. Do that work and I'll do my work."

And the tree would be right. A great majority of the time, we can't blame the fruit. It's only as good as the soil ingredients. It is true that the tree's function and purpose has failed, which is why the owner in Jesus' parable could say, "Cut it down! Why should it use up the soil?" God can certainly say that about our failures as well. But the man taking care of the vineyard, who represents Jesus advocating on our behalf before a righteous God, suggested that changing the treatment of the soil was the real solution. It all starts with the soil.

On a broader level, the story is a picture of what living a life of good deeds, performance, and striving to be better is like. It doesn't work. The story shows why the law given in the Old Testament failed to fix what was broken and sinful in us, and why Jesus had to sacrifice himself to reconcile us. If yelling at the fruit or trying harder were the answer, then the Bible would have ended at Exodus 20, after the Ten Commandments, with a statement like, "Make sure you do these ten, and have a nice life." But most of the Bible is about the failure of trying harder and how much we need God's grace. Working harder could not work and did not work, so there had to be another solution. "What the law was powerless to do because it was weakened by the flesh, God did by sending his own Son in the likeness of sinful flesh to be a sin offering" (Rom. 8:3).

Think about our tradition of new year's resolutions. We make a commitment to lose weight, eat right, work out more, get the new job, have better devotionals, make a marriage better, find a great dating relationship. We are serious about it and it's not a joke. And we dedicate ourselves to it for a while. But as we all know, the great majority of the time those commitments don't make it very far into the year. Crummy fruit takes more than just dedication to repair.

There are certainly things we can change. These tend to be minor issues that haven't been plaguing us for a long time. Your voice might be too loud, or you might have a tendency to slump your shoulders. Most often, a few reminders can fix that. But for the things that count in life and have been long-standing and serious, yelling at the fruit will simply not get the results you want.

This is true in our personal lives as well as in our business lives. In my work as a family coach, I had a husband, Sean, tell me that he had an anger problem. His wife, Rachel, agreed. They both felt that he overreacted to frustrations and stayed mad longer than was good for him or anyone around him.

They had a daughter who had been a longtime addict and whose behavior had negatively impacted the family for years. When the topic came up, Sean would become irritated, angrily saying things like, "She squandered everything we gave her" and "She doesn't want to get well and doesn't care about how she has been affecting us."

When Rachel would bring up the anger, Sean wasn't defensive. He would say, "I know, I should get over it." But nothing much would change. So he asked me one day for some techniques.

"Like what?" I asked.

"You know, like patience or prayer or deep breathing or something."

"Have you tried these?"

"Yes."

"My experience has been that if it's a significant problem and it hasn't gone away with techniques like these, there's something underneath the surface [read: let's go to the soil]. So let's talk more about how your daughter's behavior has impacted you."

Long story short, Sean felt totally helpless about his daughter. A very successful businessman, he had been able to solve tremendous problems and conquer many mountains. But he could not influence his daughter to stay off drugs.

Sean, like a lot of high-performing professionals, was much more comfortable with expressing his frustration and anger than with showing his vulnerability and sadness. So the anger served to protect him from the discomfort of being vulnerable.

I focused on helping him to be more open and vulnerable, and we dug around the soil of his childhood and his past. We had him talk with healthy people who loved and accepted him, putting good nutrients into him. It was hard work, but in time he became more comfortable, or integrated, with his vulnerability. The result was that while he still felt anger and could use it to take action to solve a problem, he was now able to feel sad and helpless about his daughter and be comforted by God, his wife, and his friends.

Sean didn't need techniques to change his emotional fruit. He needed a different way of relating, and the soil changes made all the difference.

The same was true of Dylan, the sales SVP. Though he had thought he just needed to concentrate on being with his directs more, we found a different answer. Dylan was insecure as a sales manager. He didn't feel nearly as accomplished and competent in this role as he did in his role as a salesman, which came to him naturally. So his behavior would always default to working more with his clients rather than developing his people. Fortunately for Dylan, this was not a deep or difficult fix. We enrolled him in a good leadership training program, in which he acquired the necessary skills. Soon he was spending the right amount of time with his salespeople to help them succeed, and the results were excellent.

CHAPTER 4

THE TRUNK OF CHARACTER

The fruit of a tree cannot exist suspended in air. It rests on and is supported by the trunk. One of the main functions of the trunk is to transport nutrients upward to supply the fruit with what is necessary for growth. The trunk must be strong enough to keep the elements and disease out and to help the tree stand upright in weather. In the path of growth, the trunk is your character, performing the same functions

When we think of the word character, it brings to mind aspects such as honesty and moral fiber. We think of people who are truthful and upright. However, there is another meaning of character, which, while it includes honesty and uprightness, is more broadly about our internal life and how it expresses itself. Here is my definition: character is that set of capacities required to meet the demands of reality. Reality dictates how we use our time and energy, laying out our responsibilities to follow God, be kind to others, solve problems and challenges, make a living, handle our finances well. These are simply the requirements of life.

To meet these common demands and be successful, we must equip ourselves with the necessary capacities to get the job done. A surgeon must be equipped with the knowledge and skill to operate on her patient. Knowledge and skill are her capacities. Without them, she would not be competent in her task.

And generally speaking, our life's success or lack of success often depends on how well our character capacities are working, how strong and developed they are. The Greek word for character in Romans 5:3–4—"Not only so, but we also glory in our sufferings, because we know that suffering produces perseverance; perseverance, character; and character, hope"—can be translated as "experience." As we grow and develop through tough times, we become experienced in life, relationships, tasks, and obstacles. An experienced person is an equipped person, ready to tackle life.

You will find this definition underlying most of my books and the books that Dr. Henry Cloud and I write, as it is foundational to an understanding of how people grow and succeed personally and professionally.

We all need the four quadrants of nutrients (which we will cover in the next section) applied to each of the four character capacities that form the trunk of character. These capacities are bonding, boundaries, reality, and capability.

1. Bonding. This is the ability to have deep, healthy, meaningful relationships with God and people. Another, more technical description is "need-based attachment." Bonding is much more than having friends, though all good friendships have bonding. It is being able to express vulnerability with one another and meet each other's needs. People who can be open, trusting, and vulnerable with others and can elicit openness, trust, and vulnerability from others are able to navigate the world of relationships more competently. They live in the atmosphere of love and connection. Jesus said, "My command is this: Love each other as I have loved you" (John 15:12). Those who have a hard time in this area tend to struggle in love, romance, family, and work relationships.

2. Boundaries. This is your capacity to know what is and what is not yours to own or take care of. We have only so much time, energy, and resources, so we need to know what to say yes to and what to say no to. We need to know where others end and we begin. And we need to know how to approach others to confront issues in direct but caring ways. This is the essence of all of my *Boundaries* books, and it can be summarized in Proverbs 4:23: "Above all else, guard your heart, for everything you do flows from it." People who have a healthy capacity in the area of boundaries are able to guard their hearts—their values, thoughts, feelings, and choices. Those who have a weak boundaries capacity often struggle with going too far in taking responsibility for the hearts of others, which is called codependency or enabling.

3. Reality. Reality is best described as what is or what exists. There are two types of reality: positive and negative. Positive reality is what we all want: positive outcomes, positive relationships, and positive thinking. Negative reality—loss, failure, sin, brokenness—is more difficult to deal with. Not only that, but negative reality has three components: the negative aspects of ourselves, the negative aspects of others in our lives (someone treating you poorly or judging you unfairly), and the negative aspects of the world at large (global poverty and disease).

People who can live with both the positives and the negatives are able to let go of their losses, learn from their failures, and move on. They live in forgiveness with others. "Be kind and compassionate to one another, forgiving each other, just as in Christ God forgave you" (Eph. 4:32). Those who have a hard time in this capacity try to avoid negative reality through perfectionism (trying too hard never to make a mistake), self-condemnation (negative self-talk after failure), blaming others, or just trying to think positive and ignore half of reality!

4. Capability. This capacity is about being prepared to function in the world of adults. It encompasses the ability to be on mutual ground with other grownups, rather than relating as an approval-seeking child, a reactive adolescent, or a controlling parent. It involves learning what your gifts and talents are, and your mission and life's purpose, in which you express those talents. It provides a persevering stick-to-it work ethic. And it has to do with a healthy perspective on sexuality.

Individuals who are mature in these areas have the ability to make success in life happen and can move into love, marriage, career, and service to others. "Brothers and sisters, stop thinking like children. In regard to evil be infants, but in your thinking be adults" (1 Cor. 14:20). Those who struggle here often have trouble in navigating mature relationships and being fulfilled in their careers.

THE TRUNK NEEDS SUPPORT
TO SUPPORT THE FRUIT

You can easily see how a strong trunk, able to convey the necessary nutrients, contributes to healthy fruit, and how the reverse is true. A client of mine, Danielle, who had some deficits in the boundaries capacity, had great difficulty saying no to Lauren, her adult daughter. Lauren was a young wife and mother who called or texted her mom at least once a day, and often more, with marriage and parenting challenges. As a dutiful mother, Danielle thought it was her job to support, encourage, and advise her daughter. In effect, however, she was staying in the role of Lauren's life support system. Though she wasn't cooking her meals or checking her homework, Danielle was keeping Lauren from taking ownership of developing her own relational support system.

The problem was that the more Danielle supported, the more Lauren asked for, as she was becoming more and more dependent on her mom's warmth and wisdom rather than relying on her friends or herself. And who wouldn't, really? Mom is the one who knows you and accepts you, and you don't have to explain yourself a lot for her to understand you.

To Danielle's chagrin, she began to feel resentful of her own daughter. She told me, "I love Lauren, but I'm starting to dread seeing her texts, because I know it will be another long conversation about her problems, and I'm getting burned out." That is a clear example of a bad people fruit, caused by a weak boundaries capacity. No one should feel that way about one's adult child.

I said, "Let's realize first that you are contributing to your burnout, because you are Lauren's first responder, like the firemen who enter a blazing house. She comes to you with her struggles before she does the leaving and cleaving that the Bible teaches, because you are much easier to bring into her world. You have known her from birth, you are warm, she trusts you, you are patient and considerate with her rambling, and you have great answers. When I'm having challenges, I'd like to call you too!"

She said, "Okay, that's probably true. What do I do?"

"Here is a simple fix that will begin solving the issue. Tell Lauren, 'I'm now number four. I need for you to call three of your close friends with your struggles before you bring me into it. I think most of the time, you and your friends will support each other and come up with solutions. But I'm around if your conversations with them don't help.'"

Danielle tried it, and Lauren said, "I don't have any friends who are as helpful as you."

Danielle had the wherewithal to say, "Maybe it's time for you to find some great friends. I'm happy to help you brainstorm who that might be."

It was weird between the two of them for a while, but in time the stress in their relationship, and Danielle's helicopter parenting fatigue, resolved.

Here's a simple formula: strong trunk, great fruit; weak trunk, struggling fruit. That is why, when psychologists describe a person's underlying issues, they refer to "character structure problems." It is the same understanding. (For a more in-depth view of these four capacities, please refer to my book *Hiding from Love* and Henry Cloud's book *Changes That Heal*.)

However, every tree must have access to the right nutrients for any of this to work. The ground must be fertile with good and healthy ingredients (recall the worker's offer to "dig around" and "fertilize" the soil). And that leads us to the last aspect of the Growth Tree, the soil.

CHAPTER 5

THE SOIL INGREDIENTS

Danielle's weakness in the boundaries capacity didn't occur in a vacuum, just as Lauren's overdependency on Danielle had its roots in how Danielle related to her. Danielle had her own mom when she was a little girl. However, Danielle's mom tended to be a very different mom than the one Danielle became. Danielle's mother was clingy and dependent. She was often overwhelmed by her marriage, her kids, and her life in general. Danielle learned to be highly responsible, a good listener, and a problem solver, so she could help her mom feel supported.

As you can imagine, Danielle's training in taking care of her mom was a direct line to how she parented Lauren. To survive, she enabled Mom, and enabling became the model for most of her relationships, not just with her kids.

But there is more to it than that. Danielle was denied some essentials that she needed for her own character growth. She was not provided with a mom's love for her own needs and weaknesses, empathy for her painful feelings, and validation that it was okay not to always be on top of things. Her mom was a nice person but was neglectful of some of the core nutrients Danielle required. And the result was, Danielle entered her parenting years with no sense of her own needs, her own boundaries, or her own self-care. She had to learn all that during the course of being a mom, and though it was successful work, it was hard work. She had to take in the right essentials from the right soil to grow strong enough and healthy enough to bear the right kind of fruit.

And that sums up the point of this entire book: to the extent that we receive the right nutrients, we bear the right fruit in life. Instead of yelling at the fruit, help yourself and help those you live with or work with to dig deep, identify what is needed, and take in the proper elements of growth. God provides three basic elements for us.

1. GRACE

Grace is a major provision and gift from God. It did a much better job than the law did to bring us into right standing before God, "so that, just as sin reigned in death, so also grace might reign through righteousness to bring eternal life through Jesus Christ our Lord" (Rom. 5:21). Another word for grace is favor, as in one person bending or stooping to be kind to another. A practical way to understand grace is to think of it as God being for us. He always wants our best and does not move to our detriment. Even when we are weak or straying or rebellious, God is for us.

Grace helps us feel loved and connected, helps us tolerate our own failure and that of others, and strengthens us to fight another day. God provides us with grace vertically (directly, from himself) and horizontally (indirectly, through people). And many types of nutrients come via grace.

Our family has close friendships with several other families. Over the years, we have spent many hours and days together. We've been on vacations and trips with them, celebrated birthdays, transitions, and achievements, and engaged in many types of events.

While we were on vacation with one of those families, I was having coffee with one of the daughters, Erin, who was in college. She told me, "I'm having a hard time."

"Sorry to hear that," I said. "What's going on?"

"Well, for starters, I'm a senior communications major in college, and I'll be looking for a job in five months, with no prospects."

"Wow, this is not an easy time for you. And you said this is for starters?"

"And Jason and I broke up."

"Oh no, that's really tough. I loved that guy. We went to dinner with him and thought things were great. No?"

"Long story," she said. "Yes, they were great, but it's really over. I am really sad and I miss him a lot."

"Those are two very hard things to deal with."

Erin sighed. "And there's another thing."

"On top of these?"

She nodded. "I don't know if I believe in God anymore."

My heart sank. Erin had been raised by Christian parents who were serious about the faith and lived it out in their parenting and their lives. "What happened?"

"Well, I go to a large university, and I have met lots of people who have lots of different ideas about religion. Plus, I have taken some classes on religion and spirituality. It's made me think a lot and question a lot. Right now, I'm not sure I truly believe, or if I've just taped Mom and Dad's beliefs onto my head. Maybe it's not really my faith but some form of theirs."

"Wow, Erin. These are some difficult and serious stressors you're having to manage nowadays. How can I help?"

"Fix my mother."

I couldn't follow the turn in the conversation. "Fix your mother? What does that mean?"

"I can't talk to her," Erin said.

"Like how?" I asked.

"Well, when I try to tell her how I'm doing with all this, she stops me and says, 'Honey, listen to me. You are smart and you are strong. You'll be okay.'"

"And how do you respond to that?"

"I ignore her. It's not really a conversation."

"Is it the same with your dad?"

"Oh no. Dad and I talk about this stuff all the time. We're fine."

"I think I understand," I said. "So you want me to help your mom handle what you're dealing with in a better way."

"Yes, fix her."

On our vacations, there are generally a few designated locations where the more serious talks happen. Here it was the back yard near the swings. I asked Katherine, Erin's mom, if we could chat there.

We arrived at the swings, and I said, "Erin's really struggling."

Katherine was concerned and serious. "Yes, she is."

"Job problems, boyfriend problems, and faith problems are a lot at one time."

She agreed.

I said, "She tells me that when you guys talk, you say she needs to realize she is smart and strong and that she'll be fine."

"Yes, that's what I tell her."

"She says it's not working and she ignores what you are saying."

"That's what happens. She does ignore me. Fix my daughter."

Now I was stuck firmly in the middle, between two people I was supposed to fix. And it was my vacation time!

Katherine said, "You're a psychologist. Help her to be able to receive my advice so she can feel better."

I thought for a moment. "I understand what you're asking, but I don't think that's what's going on here."

"I just want to encourage her and give her good advice," Katherine said. "What's wrong with that?"

"Look at it this way. Your daughter has fallen down a well. It's very deep and very dark there. It's the well of no job, no boyfriend, and maybe no God. And she is scared and overwhelmed. As her mom, you love her and want to help. So you stand at the top of the well and call down. From your vantage point, the sky is blue and the weather is fine. You say, 'Honey, you're strong, you're smart, and you'll be okay,' but she tunes you out."

Katherine nodded, so I continued.

"However, Kevin sees Erin at the bottom and he jumps in. He hugs her and says, 'Yes, it's really overwhelming and confusing and scary. But I've got you. And I'll be with you until you find your way out.' I think that may be why she feels more connected to him than she does with you."

Katherine is nobody's fool. "You want me to jump into the well."

I nodded. "You're a mom and you're a leader and you love your daughter."

"But this is hard for me. I am more of an encourager and helper. I try to solve problems and give good advice, and this isn't my natural bent."

I said, "Yes, you're very good at encouraging and helping, and Erin does need that. But your sequence is wrong."

"What do you mean?"

"Jesus came full of grace and truth to give us both, to save us and grow us. But the order is significant here. The Bible doesn't say that he came full of truth and grace; it's the other way around. It's a good illustration of how growth happens. We need to experience grace before we are ready for truth. If you've ever been 'truthed' by someone, without grace, even if they were right about what they were saying to you, it probably felt harsh, unloving, and impossible to respond to." I saw she was following. "That is why grace is so helpful. One of the functions of grace is to help us digest and metabolize the truth. Then we can make use of someone's advice without feeling judged. When we know they are truly with us, we are more prone to respond to the truth."

Katherine was thoughtful. "So getting in the well with Erin is providing grace."

"Yes, I think that is one way people 'grace' each other. But we all have to earn the right to give someone the truth, unless there is some crisis with no time to talk, like if they are standing in the road in front of a speeding car."

Katherine sighed heavily. "You don't know how hard this is for me."

"I think it will be very hard, at least at first. It's a different skill set than encouragement, help, and advice. It's more about empathy and attuning to someone's emotional state. But you can learn it."

Several weeks after that, I was talking to Erin and asked how things were going.

"My life situation is still really hard," she said. "But it's better with Mom and me now."

I knew Katherine had done the hard work of learning the additional skill of attunement, and it was helping.

I have seen this principle work in leadership teams, in mentoring, in marriages, in families, and in church. We were designed to need someone with us. Brené Brown has also used the concept of jumping into the well with someone to illustrate the power of empathy, and there's an excellent short animated video that's slightly different from my conceptualization. It is worth checking out on YouTube (search "Brené Brown on empathy").

As you read this story, you might be thinking, *I am overbalanced on advice giving and encouragement. I need to get into people's wells more.* And that's probably true; most of us need to grow in that area.

But for a moment, put that idea aside and ask yourself this question: "Who am I inviting into *my* well?" Who are you letting in? Who are you telling how you really feel about your career struggle, your relationship difficulties, or your personal life, without going immediately for a three-step solution and an encouraging word? When you can become comfortable with having people support you with grace in this manner, that is what being vulnerable is all about. And the more it becomes part of your life, the better you can dispense grace to others.

That is why grace is such an essential element for your Growth Tree. Later in the book, I'll go over several aspects of grace that form the relational nutrients. They will then travel up the trunk of your character to grow healthy fruit for your life.

2. TRUTH

Truth is simply what is factual and real. It is what is. Truth informs, educates, enlightens, corrects, and confronts us. Every time you drive across a bridge, you are trusting the truths of the laws of physics and engineering which the construction was based on. When you read a book that gives you a new way to think, you are experiencing truth.

There are many ways we can take truth into our minds and lives, among them:

- ▶ *The Bible,* which informs and guides us
- ▶ *Research,* the systematic analysis leading to truthful conclusions and principles about medicine, careers, sports, families, and theology
- ▶ *Experts,* those individuals who have high levels of data about their subject
- ▶ *Feedback,* the personal insights and observations that people who know us well tell us to help us grow and be better people

This last example, feedback, can be very powerful in a person's life. Feedback can be positive and affirming, and it can be corrective or challenging. In the Townsend Leadership Program, one of the exercises our team members engage in is called "Affirmations and Challenges," the purpose of which is to point out areas of growth and change they have observed, as well as areas of future growth. Prior to the day of the exercise, all members write out a few sentences for each fellow member. They put down some thoughts which are affirmative and some which are challenging.

Then, on the day of the exercise, the members sit in a circle with their sheets or digital devices in hand. The director picks the first person who is to receive the feedback. One at a time, each team member turns toward that member, looks them in the eyes warmly, and goes over their statements. Here are some examples.

Affirmations

- ▶ "I have been encouraged by how vulnerable you have been about yourself and your struggles."
- ▶ "I appreciate how you are all in about your personal and professional growth."

- ▸ "Your care for the other team members has been an inspiration to me."
- ▸ "You have become such a better spouse and parent since the program started."

Challenges

- ▸ "I am concerned that you are putting off some difficult decisions in your business that are going to cost you. I'd like you to address that, and we'll support you."
- ▸ "You seem to have a hard time opening up about what's really going on with you; it's mainly that you're fine and everything is good. I don't feel I really know you, and I'd like for you to talk more about your challenges."
- ▸ "You are really hard on yourself and beat yourself up when you struggle. I hate to see that, and I know it's not good for you. I'd like to help you be kinder to yourself."
- ▸ "It seems that your work is taking a great deal of time and energy from your family, and I'd like to address that with you. Maybe there are some ways you can balance things better."

We all need the truth, from its various sources, to be the people we were designed to be. But let's face it, most of us are more comfortable with receiving grace than with hearing truth. We don't wake up in the morning thinking, *It will be an awesome day if people confront me with a lot of truth.* We may value truth, but there's also an ouch factor. That is one reason grace is so important, as it delivers enough safety and acceptance for us to be able to digest the truth.

Remember that truth without grace can be judgment and condemnation. But grace without truth can become licentiousness and irresponsibility. God requires both elements.

Sometimes you need to have the grace in place prior to delivering the truth, especially when it's a tough conversation or a new relationship. In long-term and sound relationships, not as much. If you have been married twenty years and must say, "I just want you to know that I accept you" before you tell your spouse it bugs you that they don't put the cap on the toothpaste, you have a problem!

Also, grace should be a seasoning you add during a truth talk as much as something you do beforehand. We have what psychologists call a persecutory judge in our heads. That judge looks for opportunities to see others as condemning us when they are just shooting straight with us. And during a difficult conversation, the persecutory judge can get activated and derail the talk. You may have experienced this in a conversation when halfway through, out of the blue, the person says, "You're just putting me down," when you are trying to build them up through observing a problem.

So make sure, when you are in truth mode, that you make efforts to be warm, give good eye contact, let the person know you are for them, and admit that you are also flawed and need correction in your life. That will help the process.

The third element, time, shows where grace and truth combine for growth.

3. TIME

Time is a sequential process of events. It is simply the path of how life moves and how we accomplish our tasks. Milliseconds, minutes, hours, days, years, centuries, and millennia measure the passage of time and are how we measure our priorities.

Individuals who do well in life tend to be accountable to time. They are aware of it and of how little we have in life, so they order their days so as to make the most of them. "Teach us to number our days, that we may gain a heart of wisdom" (Ps. 90:12).

One of the most important uses of this prioritizing is to utilize time as the oven of growth. In this oven, various aspects of grace and truth are heated up, mixed, and melded. The outcome is a dish that is superior to the original, uncooked ingredients.

Growth and change—real and substantive change—tends to take

longer than we anticipate. We are an impatient species, and we much prefer a microwave oven approach. But if we allow God's process to work, growth happens in its correct season.

You will also find that at different seasons in your growth, you will require more of one ingredient than another. Suppose you want to go to the next level in your career and make the move you have been needing to make—let's say, to start your own small business. The first thing you will probably do is dive into the information and do tons of research, scouring books, journals, and websites. At this point, truth is the focus, because you don't even know what you don't know. It's just due diligence. But at the juncture where you now know what you don't know, you could also notice that you need support around you: people to encourage you, keep you motivated, and keep you on track. That will involve adding grace in the form of the right relationships to help you continue along the path.

Success is built around experiencing the right amounts and the right kinds of grace and truth over the right amount of time. Some combination of these three is almost always the answer to solving a problem or creating an opportunity. And it is our responsibility to figure that part out, for our own challenges, goals, and dreams.

Skills for Growth

1. Reviewing the Growth Tree, determine which of the three Ps of fruit you wish for better results in your life. Write them down, and why that is important to you.
2. Move down to the trunk of character. Which of the four capacities would help you most in developing better fruit?
3. Finally, write down where you are most deficient: in grace, in truth, or in spending the right amount of time improving what is going on.

These questions will help you focus on what you want in life, as we begin to look at the next section, which has to do with the nutrients, or fuel, that we derive from relationships.

PART 2

THE NUTRIENTS

As a certified food lover, I confess that I am not, by preference, a healthy eater. If a meal tastes great and is also good for me, I'll eat a ton. If it tastes great and isn't so good for me, same deal. If it doesn't taste great and is good for me or isn't good for me, I shy away from it and find something else to do.

But I have learned and changed over the years, and I'm putting more thought into what I'm putting into my system. As a result, I am taking risks on things that may not be uberdelicious, but if they are okay and healthy, I'll eat them.

We all know the six categories of nutrients necessary for survival, the ones you read about all the time: protein, carbs, fats, vitamins, minerals, and water. All of the nutritional science comes down to finding the best combinations of these to consume for optimal health and longevity.

We also know that whatever normal meals can't provide, supplements can make up the difference, which is why we take our capsules of vitamins and minerals. They complete the regimen of the six kinds of nutrients we need. When we ingest what we are supposed to, we have the foundation for good health.

The same is true of our personal growth and brain health. There are nutrients from relationships—the right relationships—which are just as critical to us as those from the physical world. The roots of the Growth Tree draw nourishment from soil that is full of the right sorts of nutrients. With the right amounts of these, we think clearly, feel energy, and make good decisions. When we are in deficit, we don't think well, we feel distressed, and our judgment is impaired.

In this section, you will find the four categories, or quadrants, of relational nutrients that we need, as well as the specific nutrients which compose each category. Just as there are thirteen vitamins and close to four thousand minerals, there are several relational nutrients for each of the four quadrants. The total relational nutrient count is twenty-two, divided among the four categories.

I have developed this system of relational nutrients over many years of study and working with leaders and people in general and through corresponding research into neuroscience, performance studies, clinical findings, and the Bible. The four quadrants and the twenty-two nutrients have held up over many instances of helping people to optimize their lives, their relationships, and their leadership and expand their capacity to solve problems and challenges.

CHAPTER 6

WHY THE NUTRIENTS ARE VITAL

Before we get to the nutrients themselves, it's important that you understand a few things about why they are critical to growth and success.

A large part of what I study in finding out how to develop people and organizations is in the world of neuroscience, the science of how the brain operates. As we learn more and more about the brain, we are gaining so many critical insights into how we think, choose, succeed, love, meet challenges, and grow. One of the reasons I love this area is because I have found so many well-done research studies that affirm the Bible's principles of growth. It's like seeing the canvas of a great painting, and now the artist's name is on the bottom right corner, and he finally gets the credit.

One of the most important conclusions is that the brain's structure, its operating system, can be affected by experiences, the apps it works with. Scientists have found that how the neural pathways deliver chemicals from one place in the brain to the other and how the brain processes information are both influenced by experience.

We now know that when an individual has had a highly negative experience—anything from a business failure to an emotional trauma—they have both an objective memory and a subjective memory of the experience. The objective memory is the facts surrounding the event, and the subjective memory consists of the painful emotions associated with the event. These emotions can demoralize and defeat that individual and keep them stuck, unable to move on.

Research has discovered that the right elements of a conversation with the individual can make all the difference in helping them. There are two aspects to this. First, the person helping affirms the negative reality of what happened and does not minimize or distort it. Second, the person provides a new and healthier emotional experience for the individual. When that occurs, the objective memory is preserved but the distressing subjective memory is stripped away, and healthier emotions are layered on, freeing the individual and motivating them to live more positively and with higher energy.

Let's say a salesperson doesn't handle a prize account well and loses it. The objective memory is the facts: he didn't attend to the client's needs in time to preserve the business relationship. The subjective memory is shame, guilt, and a sense of defeat.

We know that shame, guilt, and defeat can paralyze a person; it does no good for him or the organization. So when a competent boss analyzes what happened, he is best served by doing two things. He affirms the facts: "Yes, the loss of the account is your responsibility, and it was a significant failure." But then instead of heaping on more shame, guilt, and defeat, he says, "I understand how you're beating yourself up over this. At the same time, I believe in you and your talents. I am not overly concerned about this, because I know your character. I had my own learning curve in your position, and it worked out. Let me know how I can help."

Time after time, we find that the person walks out of that meeting with a new way of thinking and feeling about the situation. Unless he has significant emotional issues and needs more help from a counselor, he is on his way to growing because of what happened.

The boss's differing perspective is called a mismatching experience. The term refers to the reality that his way of looking at the matter is at odds with how the salesman is feeling about things. And if it is a true relational experience—if it is delivered with mutual openness and warmth—it removes the unhealthy emotions and replaces them with the healthier outlook.

Looking at what happened in terms of relational nutrients, the boss transferred great ingredients such as encouragement and hope to his direct through the process.

You don't need to be a therapist to do this. The boss in this situation was a client of mine, and he had simply learned the skill. While there are many instances in which a counselor is necessary, leaders can accomplish a lot more than they think they can in this relational nutrient world. And that includes you.

Relational nutrients are essential. They aren't an option. If you miss your favorite TV show, that's a bit sad, but you aren't damaged. If you miss having enough iron, you can develop anemia. Without sufficient calcium, you can be at risk for osteoporosis. In the same way, these relational nutrients are much more than a good idea to think about when we have time to take them. When we don't intake the right amounts over the right amount of time, we risk damage: personal, relational, and work problems (back to the three Ps of fruit). And on the positive side, I have seen any number of leaders transform their entire organizations when they ingested relational nutrients in the right way.

One young CEO of an IT startup told me he was amazed that when he became a more relational person, his company's performance increased significantly. He had always been a "work smarter and harder" type of leader, not given to the relational aspects of an organization. But once he began focusing on his people, his employees started saying things like, "You inspire us to do better because you listen better." At so many levels, this is essential stuff, for personal growth, family growth, and organizational growth.

I use the term relational nutrients to drive home the reality that these aren't things you can make up in your head. They come from the outside of you, from the right kinds of relationships, from people who can dispense them to you. The different aspects of grace and truth— which is another, broader way of describing the nutrients—provided over time, come from our relationships with God and with people. That is why the horizontal that I mentioned in the previous chapter is so important. Remember that God created a system in which the vertical is not enough for us. He designed us to be fueled by his Spirit, his Word, and his people. When we truly become what I call relationally oriented, rather than self-sufficient, everything changes for the better.

We need relational nutrients daily and over a lifetime, and not as once in a while events. We can't "do the relationship thing" and have it over with, as with vaccinations that can last many years. It doesn't work that way. God did not intend for us to connect at deep and vulnerable levels at a weekend retreat and then go back to our regular lives. We need to experience and ingest the nutrients over time, over and over again, to stay healthy and productive.

Think about the last time you had a bacterial infection. The physician probably prescribed a packet of antibiotics. The regimen was that you would need to take a pill or two every day for a few days. That is what works. But if you were a very busy person, you might become impatient and just take the whole packet on day one.

You would save time, but you would probably overdose and get sicker. You would not have given your body a chance to absorb the ingredients into your bloodstream over time. That is how we are healed. We take that pill or two. The body metabolizes them and uses them to fight the infection. But since there is more infection to deal with, you supply the body with another pill the next day.

We need to ingest the helpful substances in certain amounts, at certain times, not all at once. And the same is true in the personal and relational world.

I was speaking to a group of leaders at a two-day intensive retreat. We did a lot of work on the nature of healthy relationships. They engaged with each other at deep and vulnerable levels and were surprised and moved by the breakthroughs they experienced in themselves and each other. They felt freer, more energized, and more connected than most reported having felt before.

I stayed in touch with this group. Over a year's time, I noticed a huge difference between those who took what they had learned at the retreat and applied it on a regular basis and those who simply went back to life and work and put the binder on a shelf. The first group were continually growing, succeeding in business, and improving their family lives. The second group, unfortunately, didn't see much long-term change. A couple of them were becoming fuzzy on what they had learned, as the brain forgets what it does not use. That was a sad reality. Not only had they not used the information, but the information itself was disappearing. So as you read through the nutrients categories, remember that you will need to find relational sources that can provide these nutrients regularly for the rest of your life.

We were designed to be sourcers and sourcees, givers and takers, deliverers and recipients of the nutrients. You can't provide what you have not experienced. Nor should you hoard what you have and never give it away. "Freely you have received; freely give" (Matt. 10:8). My experience of most leaders is that they are much more oriented toward learning how to provide the nutrients for others than they are toward learning how to receive the nutrients themselves. Any number of leadership books will be structured accordingly.

Just remember that you cannot give what you do not possess. If you want to attune deeply to the experiences of others, you must have experienced for yourself what attunement is. That's why schools such as the Townsend Institute for Leadership and Counseling at Concordia University Irvine require counseling for their counseling, coaching, and organizational leadership students. You must have the nutrient to give the nutrient.

INTERNALIZATION IS THE PROCESS

How does the nutrient make it into the tree's system? Psychologists have termed this internalization, meaning that humans take in, or internalize, good things from other humans, which then become a part of their own character. Just as a root draws nutrients from the soil, we are always internalizing something from those around us, whether healthy (grace, support, and wisdom) or toxic (judgment, shame, or control).

Science has discovered that we best internalize things from others through experiences. When a relationship is sufficiently important to a person that they can feel some sort of interest in and emotion toward another, the transfer can happen. Our brains need not only objective data such as facts, principles, and research but also experiential data. (My book *Leading from Your Gut* deals in-depth with these two needs of the brain.) Here are a few examples of how this can happen.

> ▶ You tell a friend that your teenage daughter is doing drugs and that you are anxious and worried about her. Your friend focuses on what you are saying. He keeps full eye contact. He is not distracted. You can see in his eyes that he is concerned for you. He says, "This is pretty scary stuff. I'm really sorry." You begin to feel a bit better, though there has been no change in your circumstances. Just knowing that he understands you at your point of vulnerability and that you are not alone with the problem helps. That's the magic of internalization.

> ▶ You are talking to your direct report, a sales manager. She is not meeting her quota and is discouraged, as are you. As you query her about the causes, you realize that she has the role clarity, the talent, and the resources. She just needs a few more atta-boys to tip the ball into the net. You look at her and say, "I just want to let you know that I get it, and I have full confidence in you for this job. I think I am partly at fault for not telling you more often how talented and competent I think you are, and I'll be better about this." She leaves the meeting more energized to succeed, as she has internalized your encouragement.

> ▶ Your husband is a workaholic and is distracted when he comes home. You work as well, and you guys have young kids. But he gives very little attention to the family. You have tried being

supportive and understanding, but nothing is changing. Finally, in a nonjudgmental tone, you say, "I need to let you know that while I am aware of how hard you work, we have a problem here. I know you are exhausted after work and need your rest, but I and the kids need your time and attention. I haven't spoken up about it, but it's really hard on us." Though it is a difficult conversation, your husband realizes you are right, and you two have a productive talk. He internalized your necessary feedback, became aware of a problem he had ignored, and responded to it.

▶ Your organization has been growing quickly and needs more infrastructure, as it is running a bit over its skis. Your boss has been promising more support staff for your division. You have asked several times, but he keeps putting you off. Finally, you grab a few minutes with him, look at him in a sincere way, and say, "I need to let you know that I am a total team player, and I want to support you and the organization any way I can. I know you are under a lot of pressure yourself. But the reality is, if you don't let me fill three new admin slots in the next thirty days, we will have some serious problems. I really need you to act on what you told me last month." Another difficult conversation, but one oriented more toward a call to action than the identification of a problem. Your boss internalized your challenge and made the changes.

As you can see, these experiences involve several factors. The person delivering the nutrient is responsible for the information itself, the right sort of eye contact, warmth, the right timing and tone of voice. The receiver must take responsibility for attending, being vulnerable about his needs and situation, and being open and receptive. And when the two individuals connect, you have internalization. This book will provide a number of examples of how this happens, as a guide to receiving and delivering the right nutrients in the right amounts at the right times.

Internalization means it becomes a permanent part of your

system. Internalization is much more than filling up the gas tank of a car. That system was designed to burn up all the fuel, and when it's gone, it's gone. Internalization certainly provides our fuel for life. People often respond almost instantly to the right sort of conversation, as in the examples cited. But that doesn't mean that a day later they will need to have the same conversation again, operating from an empty tank. That does happen when a need is severe or a person is in a crisis, but it's not a normal occurrence.

What does happen is that we take in relational nutrients which build strong and healthy character. The substances become a permanent part of us, in the same way that biological nutrients are the building blocks of our body. So while part of the usefulness lies in what is happening right now, another part helps us become the person God intended us to be all along, "built up until we all reach unity in the faith and in the knowledge of the Son of God and become mature, attaining to the whole measure of the fullness of Christ" (Eph. 4:12–13).

That's why we are responsible to ask for relational help not just in a crisis but on a regular and sustained basis for the rest of our lives. So many people shy away from going to others for their needs, until their back is against the wall. But that does not provide the growth and strength they require to be a mature and developed person. This is about a lifetime habit of growth!

You may not always notice or remember receiving a relational nutrient. These internalized experiences may stay in your memory or they may not. You most likely remember significant nutrient-providing experiences that were important to you.

I can remember, as if it were yesterday, a conversation with a friend who was a psychologist. He suggested I consider getting a doctorate in the field, because he thought I had the talent for it. His nutrient of encouragement changed the course of my life.

But we can't and don't remember every character-building experience. I have had thousands of conversations with people who built into my life and whose support, care, and wisdom are part of my sinews, and I don't remember most of them. The significant experiences, which often symbolize a greater theme, tend to remain. That was the case with the psychologist who encouraged me to train in the field, as the greater theme was that someone who was highly proficient and whom I respected saw potential in me.

So don't worry about what you do and don't remember. Just concentrate on getting the right nutrients into your system via having the right people who can supply them. I present a structure for this in part 3. The process takes care of the rest.

Absorbing the nutrients is a metabolic process. Internalizing relational nutrients is very similar to the process of metabolism that your body uses. Metabolism occurs when substances in our system are transformed so that we can use them. The body metabolizes food to create energy, strengthen itself, and heal. In the same way, we metabolize relational nutrients when we internalize them. They are converted into emotional and intellectual energy, strength, and healing.

I recently attended a large public event that a client's organization hosted. It was extremely well done, with thousands of attendees, and it was a first-class experience. Yet I noticed that my client, who was the CEO, was not in sight, nor was the name of the organization. I had expected to see one or both all over the place, as the audience would have welcomed it. He would have had a great branding opportunity.

I talked to him afterward and said, "Awesome event! Congratulations. I did have one thought: I wonder if you were somewhat guarded about showcasing your organization and yourself as being the driving engine behind all of this. I call this 'narcissism phobia,' meaning a fear of being perceived as arrogant. But I don't think you or your people are arrogant at all! Just think about it." He and I are close friends, with a solid trust relationship, so I knew that he was attending not just to my words but to all of the other signals I was conveying. I trusted that he was internalizing my concern.

He texted me later and said, "Your observation was spot-on. I talked to my team about this, and we realized that our organizational culture has been so concerned about not being showy that we have overcompensated, going too far in the other direction. We are making steps to correct this."

So the internalized relational nutrient (my observation) was then metabolized in his own head into attention, focus, and action. That is the power of relational metabolism. You can see how relational experiences like this one, whether you are on the giving end or the receiving end, make a huge difference in your life and in your leadership.

You see the process at work in the Bible as well. Paul wrote about how he and his companions experienced the faith of the believers in the Thessalonian church and how that translated into encouragement for them. "Brothers and sisters, in all our distress and persecution we were encouraged about you because of your faith" (1 Thess. 3:7). Internalizing relational experience led to a sense of personal encouragement.

There is a range of time for delivering the nutrients. It all depends on the situation. It might take five minutes and it might take a dinner. Our needs vary. When you've had a hard day and you're driving home, a few minutes of windshield time may restore your attitude. On the other hand, a complex personal matter might take several hours with someone who knows you well and wants to help you get to the bottom of things.

You are probably in deficit right now, because unfortunately the great majority of people I know and work with aren't getting the nutrients they need for growth. When I get to know them, I find that they're only marginally involved in caring for themselves, recognizing their needs, gathering the right people to provide the nutrients, and metabolizing the experiences into growth and action. They are running largely on willpower, determination, and the vertical dimension of faith.

There are several reasons for missing out on the nutrients, among them busyness, minimizing one's needs, and not wanting to be a burden to others. Whatever the reasons, you need to know that internalization and metabolization are more than a good idea, more than important; they are crucial to your life and success.

THE NUTRIENTS LIST

The twenty-two ingredients we need are each described in the next few chapters, with examples from life and leadership of how they occur in relationships. These chapters have several takeaways.

- ▶ Helping you identify which nutrients you need
- ▶ Helping you learn the skill of receiving these nutrients from others
- ▶ Helping others identify which nutrients they need
- ▶ Helping you learn the skill of providing them to others

To keep things simpler, the nutrients are organized into four categories called quadrants. Each quadrant contains several nutrients, with a common theme. Here is a brief summary of the quadrants.

- ▶ *Quadrant 1: Be Present.* Nutrients in this quadrant are high in grace and low in volume of words. They are about jumping into the well with the other person and entering that person's experience. Quadrant 1 nutrients are sometimes delivered by eye contact, body language, warmth, and kindness. When you just need someone to get it and be there with you, you are looking for a Q1 experience.
- ▶ *Quadrant 2: Convey the Good.* Quadrant 2 nutrients convey with words what is needed. They are also high in grace. Whether they help encourage someone who is down or celebrate a win, these ingredients come in statements that penetrate to the other person's heart and mind in a positive way.
- ▶ *Quadrant 3: Provide Reality.* Sometimes a person simply needs truth and information. They need someone to help them recognize or understand the data points, whether quantitative or personal.
- ▶ *Quadrant 4: Call to Action.* Quadrant 4 nutrients challenge someone to take a step toward growth or solving a problem.

They are oriented toward inducing some behavior that will help the person change what needs to be changed.

If you recall the four examples of internalization, you will see each quadrant represented in this order. Some nutrients will have aspects that could relate to a different quadrant, but the dominant purpose helps define where each nutrient works best.

In the next few chapters, the description of each nutrient is followed by a sample statement representing something you might say to someone to either provide the nutrient or request it for yourself.

The table on page 81 shows a macro view of the four quadrants and their respective nutrients.

A final word on nutrients: As you learn about these, you are likely to discover nutrients that you had no idea existed, much less knew you needed. But you will find, when you engage in this process, that you will become more of yourself, or even someone better than the you who now exists. God's process of growth through relationship is sound and affects individuals, marriages, families, and organizations.

THE FOUR QUADRANTS OF RELATIONAL NUTRIENTS

Quadrant 1: Be Present	Quadrant 2: Convey the Good
▸ **Acceptance:** Connect without judgment ▸ **Attunement:** Be aware of what another is experiencing and respond to it ▸ **Validation:** Convey that a person's experience is significant and not to be dismissed ▸ **Identification:** Share your similar story ▸ **Containment:** Allow the other to vent while staying warm without reacting ▸ **Comfort:** Provide support for someone's loss	▸ **Affirmation:** Draw attention to the good ▸ **Encouragement:** Convey that you believe in someone's ability to do the difficult ▸ **Respect:** Assign value ▸ **Hope:** Provide reality-based confidence in the future ▸ **Forgiveness:** Cancel a debt ▸ **Celebration:** Acknowledge a win, both cognitively and emotionally
Quadrant 3: Provide Reality	**Quadrant 4: Call to Action**
▸ **Clarification:** Bring order to confusion ▸ **Perspective:** Offer a different viewpoint ▸ **Insight:** Convey a deeper understanding ▸ **Feedback:** Give a personal response ▸ **Confrontation:** Face someone with an appeal to change	▸ **Advice:** Recommend an action step ▸ **Structure:** Provide a framework ▸ **Challenge:** Strongly recommend a difficult action ▸ **Development:** Create a growth environment ▸ **Service:** Guide engagement to giving back

CHAPTER 7

QUADRANT 1

Be Present

"I'M NOT ALONE IN THIS"

I was talking with Grant, a key executive in an automotive parts company owned by his boss, Brian, whom I was consulting. I had asked Grant how things were going, and he wanted to talk about Brian. He said, "He is an incredible leader, and I'm lucky to be working for him."

I asked why, and Grant said, "The best way I can explain it is by describing what happens in our weekly one-to-one meetings. We spend the first half of the time going over goals, strategy, and performance issues. Then, in the second half, Brian just looks at me and says, 'So how are you doing?' And he waits. That's my time to talk about whatever my concerns are. Sometimes I'll touch on how my team is working or a challenging client or how I think I'm fitting into the program. It can be any number of issues.

"Both halves of the meeting are very helpful for me. But the second half is probably more important. Brian won't say a lot or give me a great deal of advice about whatever I'm bringing up, unless I ask him for it. But the impact of the way he listens and how he is focused on me and what he does say really adds up. I leave our one-to-ones feeling like he's with me and he gets me. I know, whatever the situation, I'm not alone in this."

Knowing Brian well, I had also observed how he paid attention to his people, not only in the office but at home with family as well. When it was time to give advice, to provide perspective, and to challenge people to action, he was highly effective. But when a person just needed to know that he was with them in the situation, Brian conveyed that as well.

We know from neuroscience and from attachment research that a great deal of growth and health comes from simply communicating to each other that we are present with them. Just letting them know, using very few words, that they are not alone causes endorphins to be released, and the person can forge ahead in their challenges, buoyed by the connection.

By contrast, isolation is one of the most debilitating experiences we can have. Study after study has shown that, especially in times of stress, we lose focus, perseverance, and energy when we feel disconnected from others. I referred to Genesis 2:18 in chapter 1, and here again it is so clear that it's not good that we are alone. Presence comes from one another and from God. In Psalm 16, David says to God, "You will fill me with joy in your presence" (v. 11). Over and over in the Bible, God lets us know that the "being with" is important to him, for our sakes.

Think about times in your life when you have been with a person, perhaps at dinner, taking a walk, or watching the sunset, and though it's a quiet time between you two, you feel connected and maybe even content. The relational nutrients in Q1 are common in that capacity. One individual conveys to another, in body language, eye contact, tone of voice, emotional presence, and words, that she isn't all by herself in her situation. And that makes all the difference.

Of all the nutrients, those in Q1 are the most challenging for leaders to provide and receive. Leadership is about purposeful and intentional movement, about actions toward a mission and a goal. It's often hard for a leader to refrain from giving advice and direction—or asking for it—and learn how to just be with someone. It can feel useless or purposeless. And yet that's the message to all of us in Jesus' conversation with Martha and Mary (Luke 10:38–42). While Martha was certainly trying to be productive, Jesus clarified that Mary's being present with him was the better thing.

However, as with all of the nutrients, Q1 nutrients are deeply important to our individual and personal lives. When friends and families can relate on this level, people are happier and healthier. A few days ago, I had lunch with a friend who was going through some stresses with his teenage son. The son was acting out in school and was disrespectful with the family. Fortunately, my friend was being proactive and doing all of the right things. He got his family into counseling, they were learning new ways to relate, and the school was involved in healthy ways.

At the same time, it was a very stressful season for my friend. He was fatigued and, even though things were slowly going in the right direction, feeling a bit discouraged. I didn't have any advice to give him, as I thought he was doing everything he should be. So I simply listened, let him know I understood, and empathized.

I didn't think I was doing a lot to help how he felt. But at the end of our lunch, he said, "Thanks. I feel better now."

"I'm glad to hear it. You're important to me. What made you feel better?"

"Basically, you were there. I feel different inside, like someone else gets it who's on my side. I feel more ready to fight for my kid another day."

No advice. No wisdom. No solutions. But there was clearly a transfer of relational nutrients from me to my friend, and it made the difference.

You may be seeing how Q1 nutrients apply to your personal life, but you may still be a bit fuzzy about how they relate to your professional life. That's why I opened this chapter with the story of Brian and Grant, to show how relevant Q1 is. It's not some touchy-feely exercise which should be relegated to human resources. That is a very limited and ineffective way to look at it. When leaders learn to be present— really present—with others at work, they see everything get better: teams, culture, engagement, and performance. Everything wins.

For each of the six nutrients in Q1, I'll give an overview and a description. Then I'll show how you can develop the skill of providing, as well as experiencing, that valuable growth element. In addition, there will be a short sample statement, from the professional or personal world, to give you a start on this.

You will need to develop a fairly robust emotional vocabulary for Q1 and Q2, more than for the other two quadrants. These nutrients are tied up with feelings. Some people have a rich emotional vocabulary and will have no trouble using the words to deliver the nutrients. Others may have a more limited vocabulary, with words like sad, mad, and glad, and that just won't do the trick. People's emotions have nuances. Great leaders and healthy people become competent in using emotional language. In the back of this book, I have a list of more than one hundred words that you can review and incorporate into your emotional vocabulary, for use in your life and conversations.

ACCEPTANCE

Courtney, a client of mine who ran an entertainment company, hired Alex, a marketing professional, as part of her key team. As marketing and entertainment go hand in hand, Alex was a critical hire for the company, with a lot riding on him. After the orientation process, Courtney asked him to make a presentation to the team in a few days about his creative and strategic marketing ideas to help the company.

Alex froze. His anxiety spiked. He couldn't focus. He even had problems sleeping. Apparently, the combination of his performance-driven personality plus being the new kid on the block, subject to the scrutiny of the team, was a bit much for him.

They decided to postpone the meeting for a couple of weeks. Courtney even helped Alex with the prep. That seemed like the solution, until a few days before the meeting, he again went to her and said, "I don't think I'm capable of this. I am really anxious about screwing up and letting everyone down."

Courtney thought for a moment. Then she leaned over her desk toward Alex, gave him full eye contact, and said simply, "If you screw up, you're okay with me."

Alex calmed down a bit. And he asked her to repeat that brief statement, which she did, as it was very impactful for him.

Long story short, he did fine at the presentation and had a successful stint at the company. But he always referred to Courtney's words as instrumental in the launch.

This conversation is a picture of the relational nutrient of acceptance, which I define as connection without judgment: you assure the person that you are for them, even if they fail and even if you disagree. Look at what Courtney did. In very few words, along with positive body language and good eye contact, she conveyed that she accepted Alex, even if he screwed up.

I can't overemphasize this last phrase, because it is the heart of acceptance. It's easy to accept someone when we like them, when they succeed, and when we agree with them. But that is a cheap acceptance. Acceptance makes a difference only when we provide it to a judged, condemned, or insecure part of the person.

Alex was panicked about failure. Suppose Courtney had said, "You'll make it. I know you will." That is an encouraging statement, and encouragement is a Q2 relational nutrient. But it would not have comforted Alex. The proper nutrient, when a person feels judged, is that of acceptance no matter what.

All of us carry a judge inside our heads. This judge is often harsh and highly critical of us and causes damaging self-talk, such as, *There I go again; I'm a loser; I'll never make it.* That judge-driven self-talk then alters the way our brain works. Rather than operating in the rational and mature prefrontal cortex, it operates in the emotional amygdala, the part of our brain that triggers the reactions of fight, flight, freeze, or fold. Alex was operating in his amygdala. Courtney's stance of acceptance modified the judge, changed the message, and allowed Alex to perform again.

Acceptance is an important principle in the Bible as well. We are to "accept one another, then, just as Christ accepted [us], in order to bring praise to God" (Rom. 15:7). The Greek word for accept means take to oneself, in the way you welcome a friend at the airport or greet someone you haven't seen for a while. It is a word of connection and friendship. Just as we are "taken in" to God through Christ's death, we are to show acceptance in our relationships. There can be no condemnation, as we also have escaped that fate.

There is a reason why this particular nutrient is the first one in the first quadrant. It's because until we feel accepted, we cannot be vulnerable and open. Think about a time when you really let yourself down and failed miserably, and instead of accepting you, someone harshly criticized you. That is a very painful experience, and more than likely, it taught you that opening up about your negatives was not a good idea. So you shut that internal door.

Acceptance opens the door to all the rest of the relational nutrients. It helps us be vulnerable to relationships that count so we can receive nutrients from them. We all need to be on God's operating table, and acceptance is the door to the operating room. It gives us the chance for optimal growth, change, and healing.

If you want to truly accept someone, never minimize the negativity of their behavior, saying things like, "It wasn't that bad" or "You were having a bad day" or "It could have been worse." If the person really blew it and made a significant mistake or had a genuinely crummy attitude, that is just reality and needs to be acknowledged by both of you. Otherwise, the part of the person that needs to be accepted still lives in a judged and isolated state. The acceptance doesn't really penetrate the heart and help. So statements such as, "Yes, it seems like you blew it, but you and I are fine" are much more helpful.

Be like Courtney. You don't need a lot of words; it's more about being with the person. Just keep your body language "toward," your eyes friendly, and your tone warm, and tell them in some way, "Even if you have ruined things, you're okay with me and I'll help you." You don't have to approve, and you don't have to agree. But we all have to accept.

And remember the well story. In your own dark times, be courageous and ask that safe person if you're okay with them. It will set you free.

Sample: "I know you're beating yourself up over not making your quota. Sure, it's an important concern. But you and I are okay regardless, and I'll help you."

ATTUNEMENT

I was meeting with Brandon and Kimberly, a couple who ran a business together. Family businesses are complex, as you have to spin a great number of plates, including kids, relatives, employees, and your marriage. At that meeting, Kimberly was at the end of her rope. She said, "This month has really been terrible. Our kids are fighting all the time, the company is going through so many changes, and my dad is pretty sick. I just hate all of this."

Brandon, who tended to be more of a problem solver, jumped in with his advice. "Well, you need better boundaries with the kids, and we just need to give your dad's health to God. And maybe that will help you have more energy and focus for what's going on at work . . . Hey, what's wrong?"

As you can imagine, Kimberly was shaking her head. "This is what happens," she told me.

Brandon said, "What is what happens?" He was genuinely confused, because he was genuinely trying to help.

"Kimberly doesn't need answers right now," I said. "She needs you to attune to her. C'mon, try to really attune to her."

Fortunately, I had been working with this couple for a while, so Brandon knew what I meant by the word attune. He looked away for a few seconds, getting his words together. Then he looked at Kimberly with a warm expression. "Honey, sorry about how I handled this. I think with what you're going through, you must just be overwhelmed and scared and sad. It's an awful time for you."

Kimberly's face changed. She seemed to relax a bit, and her eyes glistened. "Yes. That's how I feel. Thanks." The transfer had been made, and the couple were realigned with each other.

Attunement involves three elements.

1. You become aware of another's emotional state.
2. You respond to the other person in an empathetic way.
3. The other person feels attuned to.

Attunement is being in tune with another person, the way the strings of a guitar are in tune with each other.

You may know someone who just gets you, so you don't have to explain yourself very much to them. That's what the experience is like. Attunement begins at birth, when a mother pays attention to the feelings of her child, and it continues until the day we die.

Attunement is similar to active listening and empathy. But it is more than this, because it also requires being in tune with a person as their feelings change. It takes work to stay in touch with someone who is anxious, then irritated, then sad. But the result is that the attunee feels, *I am not alone in this; someone else is here with me and gets it.* And just like my friend at the beginning of this chapter, they feel energy, positivity, and the wherewithal to take the next step to address their problem.

Jesus attuned deeply to others. Speaking to the masses, he said, "Come to me, all you who are weary and burdened, and I will give you rest" (Matt. 11:28). I have read that verse innumerable times when I've been stressed out. When I see myself described as "weary and burdened," I can't help but feel connected to Jesus. I no longer feel alone. Jesus' skill of attuning to others can become your skill as well.

Speaking of skill, sometimes a person will tell me, "I'm not a counselor; I'm a businessperson. This isn't my world." That is simply not true. Anyone can learn to deliver this relational nutrient. It just takes practice. Brandon will always be a hard-charging company owner, and that is a good thing. But he treats Kimberly, his kids, and his employees much better now because he has learned attunement.

Often, people who have not received attunement have trouble providing it, and this is true of all the nutrients. Keep bringing people into your well. Tell them, "I don't need advice right now. I would like to tell you how things are, and if you'll let me know that you get it, that's what I need." I had all sorts of great advice to tell a man about how to handle his business, but when I attuned, he said, "Well, that's really what I needed. Don't need any advice; I knew what to do. I just didn't have any gas in the tank to do it." Sometimes, however, the attuning helps the person think clearly enough to come up with their own solutions. Quadrant 1 nutrients help people move out of their amygdala and into their prefrontal cortex, where the more advanced problem-solving capacities lie.

Sample: "When your husband shut down the conversation and started watching TV, you must have felt alone and that you don't matter. I get it; that is difficult."

VALIDATION

I was at a meeting with two business partners who were at odds over a decision to hire a new COO. One partner was all for the person, and the other was very hesitant. The reserved partner didn't have an objective reason for his concern. He just said, "I've got a bad gut about this." His partner then gave several factual reasons—good resume, experience, solid interview—why this was the right hire. But the reserved partner kept saying, even more forcefully, "I've got a bad gut about this." Then the other partner would repeat his reasons.

I finally saw what was going on and said to the factual partner, "You're making him dig in his heels."

"How am I doing that?" he asked.

"I think all he needs is for you to validate that he has concerns he needs to express, even if they are gut concerns."

The hesitant partner said, "That's it!"

I asked him to explain.

He turned to his partner. "Just say that my gut matters here!"

The partner was startled but did the right thing. He said, "I'm sorry. I was pretty low-EQ with you on this. You're right, instead of tossing a lot of data at you, I should have just let you know that I think your gut matters. Because it does to me. Your gut has saved us many times."

The other partner said, "Thanks, that's all I needed. I don't know why I feel what I feel, but that will work out. I'm okay with the data points now."

This is a perfect example of invalidation, or simply not taking someone else's experience seriously. It is the opposite of validation. When we validate someone, we convey that their experience is significant and not to be minimized or dismissed. Even if we don't agree with the person's opinion or memory or reaction, a validating response still communicates that, right or wrong, it is important.

Think about the last time you told another person about a stress or loss in your life, and you heard something like the following:

- ▶ "It's not that big a deal."
- ▶ "You're overreacting."
- ▶ "Get over it."
- ▶ "It wasn't that bad."
- ▶ "Those are your emotions; think logically."
- ▶ "Just think about something else."

Most likely, these statements weren't helpful to you, and you probably felt like your thoughts and feelings were not important to the other person, and they shouldn't have been important to you either. Validation is an important Q1 nutrient. It helps us pay attention to our experiences and make sense of them so that we can make good decisions about what's going on.

When I am working with executive teams, I often encounter

the eternal friction between marketing and finance. The marketing person has sweeping creative ideas to help build the brand and sales, while the financial person is protective of the budget. This is a positive friction, and when things go right, it helps the company grow and succeed. However, part of my job is to deal with and resolve invalidation between the individuals. It goes like this:

Marketing: "I want to propose that we implement the following innovative social media and TV ads to target our new product line. I'm convinced that this will take us to the next level."

Financial: "We can't afford it."

Marketing: "You don't want the company to grow."

Now, the truth may lie in the financial person's perspective or in the marketing person's perspective, or somewhere in the middle. But that's not the point. For a team to work, each member needs to convey that the others' viewpoints matter, right or wrong. Otherwise, the invalidated person tends to go on the defensive, and the entire process can deteriorate into an argument with no winners.

So I will say something like, "Okay, you both just shut each other down, and it's going to keep us from making a good decision. Even if you disagree, I need you to let the other person know, in an authentic way, that what they think matters."

Then the financial person will say something like, "Sorry, I jumped the gun. I really do appreciate how much time you put into finding innovative ways to promote what we do. You have a great passion for pushing us."

And the marketing person will say, "Yeah, same here. I know you have saved us several times from expenditures that would have wrecked us. I appreciate how you guard the company."

After that, they can disagree all they want, and the result is generally a decision that helps the company.

Certainly there are times when we just need to get over it. We all can have a tendency to obsess and worry forever about something we can't change, and it's best to move on. Too much postgame analysis can slow us down. If you are a commercial pilot and you're having a bad day, and then your engine catches on fire, you need to get over it and get moving on solving the emergency. But in normal situations, when someone struggles, validate. You need it, and others need it from you.

Sample: "I know you think you should be happy about your daughter being in college, and you question whether it's mature to feel sad. I think it's important. I want to hear about it."

IDENTIFICATION

I was facilitating a small group of leaders who had gathered in a confidential setting to air out their work and life challenges. The leaders had various levels of experience. Cody, one of the younger members of the group, opened up about a major struggle in his marriage. Things were at the point that his wife wasn't sure she wanted to stay in the marriage, and he was broken up about it. Cody was hesitant about talking to the group, however. "I'm not sure I should be bringing this up, or even if I should have this problem," he said. "I mean, there are a lot of leaders here who are far more successful than me, and you guys have your acts together."

I said, "Sorry you're going through this, Cody. It's obviously a very hard season for you." Looking around the room, I asked, "Who wants to help him with his situation?"

Taylor, who was older and had achieved a high level of success in his career, looked at Cody and said, "In a lot of ways, you are me fifteen years ago. My wife and I were close to the edge, and we almost didn't make it. I can remember how scared I was that I might lose the marriage. And I remember how ashamed I was about all the things I had done wrong to drive her away, and here I was, a leader. We are solid now, and I'm happy to talk about how that happened. But I want you to know that I'm glad you're in this group, and I've been through some similar rough waters."

Cody looked as though a fifty-pound weight had been lifted off his shoulders. He looked more confident, and more than that, he looked like he felt he belonged. The rest of his time in the group was a period of great transformation for him, personally and professionally, and it was launched by Taylor's comments.

The relational nutrient which Taylor transferred to Cody is called identification. When someone identifies with us, they share a similar (usually negative) experience, to help us see that we are not the only one who is challenged.

The power of identification comes from what is called normalization. Normalization is the experience of realizing that you're not some strange, mutated being who is set off from the rest of humanity because of a flaw. Rather you fit in with others. You may have your history and patterns, but being flawed doesn't exclude you. When we feel normalized, our brains are able to settle into being connected and attached to others in community, and we think, feel, and behave better.

Leaders who are vulnerable with their employees about their own struggles can inspire more commitment and loyalty than can the bulletproof type who, no matter what, project positivity and confidence. We feel closer to someone when we can identify with their struggles and mistakes. It's hard to identify with Superman or Wonder Woman. They don't fail the way we fail.

One of the unique aspects of the Christian faith is that we don't have to reach up to heaven and become like God to connect with him and belong to him. Jesus did the reverse: he came down to our level, identifying with our experiences. "We do not have a high priest who is unable to empathize with our weaknesses, but we have one who has been tempted in every way, just as we are—yet he did not sin" (Heb. 4:15).

Had Cody had enough experience with the leadership group, he simply could have said, "My marriage is in deep trouble, and right now I just need to know that someone in this group can identify with what I'm going through." Not all of the members had the history Taylor had, so not everyone there could identify with Cody. But Taylor's response would have been exactly the same, without my saying anything. That's just how the transfer works. When you discover that you lack a relational nutrient, you just ask those who care about you, and the transfer is made, authentically and meaningfully.

One caveat: when someone asks you to identify with their situation (when you are Taylor), keep it short, no more than sixty seconds. Too often, the identifier will go on about their own story for a few minutes, leaving the identify-ee sitting there nodding and saying, "Wow, that was awful. So sorry you went through that." Then the one in deficit is feeling pressure to support the other person. So don't take the conversational football all the way down the field. You can say a lot in a short time, and you will help the other person. Taylor's statement took all of twenty-seven seconds.

Sample: "I understand your concern about the company's quarterly reports. I had the same thing happen a couple of years ago, and I felt like the walls were caving in. I'm with you on this one."

CONTAINMENT

I was on a business trip out of state and called Barbi from the hotel room that evening, as that is our habit on the nights we are away from each other. We talked about how our day went. I'd had a hard day with multiple stressors, including a flight delay that diverted me to a different airport, a miscommunication that caused some key people to be absent from the meeting, and a kids' travel soccer team on the same floor as my hotel room.

I vented for a while about how frustrating everything had been, and I didn't edit much. It just came out as I felt it. Then I worried that I was being selfish, burdening Barbi with my rants and bringing her down. So I said, "Sorry, is all of this stuff too much?"

She said, "No, you're dealing with a lot, but I'm okay with it. I like how we trade off our rants."

And we do trade off. We have found that it helps both of us.

This is the relational nutrient called containment. It is the act of allowing another to vent the negatives that they are feeling, without becoming overwhelmed, withdrawing, or editing the narrative. Psychologists use the term to describe how to be aware of and hold on to (contain) someone's strong and intense feelings without reacting to them. The message is, "I'm with you, and I'm fine with what you are saying and feeling. I'm strong enough to hear it, and it doesn't put me off or overwhelm me."

Containment is a highly valuable nutrient for two reasons. First, when someone contains your unedited feelings (which is not the same as being verbally disrespectful or abusive), you can make more sense of things and make better decisions. You might need someone at work (the right someone; not everyone can contain well) to just hear your frustration at the unrealistic demands of a project that has been assigned to you. When the other person can bear what you are saying, you can figure out what steps you can take to address the situation (talk to the boss, have a team brainstorm meeting, see if there are other things that can be put off).

Second, containment helps us self-regulate. Self-regulation is living with strong feelings, understanding that they are just feelings and not all of reality, and processing them so that the intensity diminishes and we can feel calm and prepared for life. Having someone contain our feelings gives us the sense that our emotions don't upset them and can be handled. In turn, we can handle our feelings as well.

The Psalms are full of examples of this kind of relationship with God, in which the writer trusts that God contains his strong and raw feelings of protest and misery. In Psalm 74:1, the writer begins with, "O God, why have you rejected us forever? Why does your anger smolder against the sheep of your pasture?" He does not walk on eggshells with how unhappy he is. Then, a few thoughts later, he says, "But God is my King from long ago; he brings salvation on the earth" (v. 12). In knowing that God is not fragile and can handle the unhappiness, the writer feels contained and restored to praise and gratitude. On a neuroscience level, he has moved from the amygdala to the prefrontal cortex, now able to self-regulate via the containment.

I was having lunch with a young owner of a new business, which was starting off small and was having major challenges with a key client, who was being very difficult. At one point, she said, "I think I just need to get very messy about how I feel about what he is doing and how it's impacting me and my company."

I said, "Sure."

For the next fifteen minutes, she let loose about her anger, her sense of helplessness and frustration, and her lack of trust in this client.

I simply listened, offered a supportive phrase here and there, and made sure she knew I was stable and okay with what she was venting out. When she was through, I said, "Yes, that's a lot to deal with. I'm glad you were able to get it out."

She said, "My head feels clearer now; all that stuff isn't causing static inside anymore. So now let's talk about solutions." And that became the second half of the lunch.

Containment doesn't take the right words as much as it requires you to be in a strong and stable place yourself. You will do others a great deal of good with it. And make sure you are being contained on a regular basis. It's good for the soul and the mind.

Sample: "You're feeling a lot of intense feelings about the situation. I'm fine with that. Tell me what's going on."

COMFORT

Most people read my books with two hats: the leadership hat and the personal hat. This is because many of the principles and skills in the material apply to both worlds. If you are wearing your personal hat right now and seeing the word comfort, you are likely to think of dealing with the loss of a loved one or of being the parent of young and vulnerable children. If you are wearing your leadership hat, you are instead likely to be a bit confused and wonder how this word fits in the world of organizations. It fits well in both contexts and is a major ingredient for growth in both.

Comfort is the relational nutrient that best addresses loss, in all of its forms. It is defined as the provision of support for someone who is experiencing a loss. Unfortunately, we experience losses in a number of ways.

- ▶ The aging and death of parents
- ▶ People we care about moving to another country
- ▶ Career mishaps
- ▶ Health issues
- ▶ Financial reversals
- ▶ Loss of dreams in a marriage
- ▶ Executive teams that dissolve
- ▶ Children whose losses magnify our own
- ▶ Losses from our own childhood

We were not designed to lose, and we are not born with the skills to deal with our losses. They must be learned. It would be debilitating to live in a permanent state of loss, having the feelings and memories associated with that loss always front and center in our brains.

The best steps we can take are the following:

- ▶ *Connect.* Talk to supportive people about the loss.
- ▶ *Grieve.* Allow yourself to express sadness over the loss.
- ▶ *Learn lessons.* Identify what can be learned in this experience, even if the situation is senseless.
- ▶ *Adapt.* Determine the ways you will function and relate in the wake of the loss.
- ▶ *Move on.* While keeping the memory and honor of the person or situation intact, begin to live the best, healthiest, and most productive life possible.

The second step, grieving, requires the nutrient of comfort. The purpose of comfort is to help someone grieve well. Grief, the expression of sad feelings, needs the right kind of relational support to resolve itself. When we grieve, we are honoring and saying goodbye, both intellectually and emotionally, to that which is no more. Grief allows us to say our goodbyes over a period of time and to then make room for God to place new people, new opportunities, and new dreams inside our minds. When we grieve, we never forget the person or situation. We place them in their proper location, in our memories, so that they can be appreciated, remembered, and loved. When grief is done well, the loss no longer dominates our thoughts. It is a part of us but not all of us.

Comfort is the relational nutrient which, more than any other, facilitates the grief process. It is a Q1 nutrient because it involves fewer words than most of the others. It requires presence and authentic care. Think of it this way: grief, by definition, places you in a state of without. You are emotionally aware and sad that you are without that person or situation. To be without feels like being alone. Comfort provides a with, so that you can bear the loss. It does not bring what is lost back to you. But it does create an emotional presence which helps you tolerate and work through the loss.

How do we comfort? Here are the elements you need in order to learn this as a skill.

- ▶ *Let the person lead.* If they want to weep about their loss or talk about the person or change the subject to some current event to give themselves a break, let them do it. Don't impose your agenda on them. Let them express whatever needs to be expressed.
- ▶ *Move toward sadness.* Be comfortable with sadness and convey that. Show by your posture, tone of voice, facial expressions, and words that you are not put off by sadness; rather you are even more there for them.
- ▶ *Refrain from attempting to change their feelings.* Don't try to cheer them up ("Look on the bright side"), teach a lesson ("You are learning to be strong"), identify ("I understand how you feel;

I've been there," sometimes helpful but rarely), or give advice ("Get back into life and do some fun things"). These statements may be helpful in some other context, but not now. They will serve only to alienate the person or cause them to judge their sadness as inappropriate and cover it with shame, preventing it from ever being resolved.

▶ *When you do speak, attune to the sadness.* Provide the attunement nutrient, focusing on letting them know you are following that emotion: "This is a real loss"; "It's very sad"; "He was important to you"; "You miss them a great deal."

You will do a great deal of good to those in your life who are dealing with loss. However, if you are reading today with your leader hat on, you may wonder about the applicability of comfort in the workplace. There is a great deal of help here.

The work environment is not a context for deep grief and comfort, as would be a friendship or a support group outside of work. Work is about performance and is a structure for getting meaningful tasks accomplished. However, people experience losses all the time at work. Someone will lose an account, lose a bid on a project, not reach a quota, or lose a position. They will have feelings about this, and those feelings should not be ignored. In addition, people can't turn off their feelings about their personal losses when they walk into the office. The leader who does not provide some way to appropriately comfort someone who is in a state of loss, even if for just a few minutes, is at risk for having team, cultural, engagement, and turnover problems. I mean, how would you feel if you were bummed out, beating yourself up, and sad about not reaching a goal, and your boss said, "Sorry, no place for these sorts of feelings; take it to HR or take it home." That's ridiculous and it wouldn't help. So here are some things you can do instead.

▶ *Go one-to-one.* If you notice someone at work who is disconsolate or looks sad, go to your walk-around-management approach and invite them to your office for a few minutes.

▶ *Ask them about themselves.* Simply say, "I couldn't help but notice that you seem to be down or sad. Would you like to talk about it?" If they would rather not, respect their boundary and let them know the invitation still stands if they decide to later. But most people will talk about what's causing the sadness.

▶ *Attune to the feelings of loss.* Let them know that you are tuning in to the emotions. This doesn't have to be anything long or protracted. It's just a warm and kind gesture.

▶ *Ask how you can help.* Work is about behavior and doing, and so, more than in the personal world, ask if there is anything practical you can do. Do they need advice or direction or a break?

▶ *Get back to work.* Again, this is not a long conversation, unless it's a serious situation. You aren't having a counselor session; you are a boss who cares. Keep it brief and let them get back. The impact of a leader who took time from their busy schedule to focus on supporting and comforting a direct will, I assure you, be noticed and appreciated.

Also, remember that often leaders are not well versed in the area of comfort, because they don't want to appear weak. However, my experience in working with some very healthy companies is that when a leader is comfortable with this part of life, people think more of them.

In addition, when losses are attended to with comfort, it restores a person's focus, concentration, and energy. You are helping your work environment by allowing a space for this important aspect of life. If the word *comfort* feels out of place to you, then just substitute *support*. And remember that we have a Savior who was "acquainted with grief" (Isa. 53:3 NASB).

Sample: This one pertains to the personal world: "I am really feeling sad about my mother's dementia worsening. I'm losing her, and it's awful. I just need you to be here with me and support me."

Even though Q1 relational nutrients are vital to health and growth, they are the least understood and least used of all the nutrients, or the least well-used. It takes a bit of work to enter someone else's experience, to convey with your tone, expression, and body language that you are present, and to be sparing with words. On the flip side, it takes courage to ask someone for one of these nutrients instead of asking for advice and suggestions. But the payoff is great. In the next chapter, you'll learn about Q2 nutrients, which are more about what you can say that can help others and yourself.

CHAPTER 8

QUADRANT 2

Convey the Good

"I AM MORE POSITIVE"

I was meeting with the young adult children in a family business to help prepare them to move into positions of leadership in the organization. One of the training exercises that I conduct in these situations involves giving the siblings a handout in which I ask them to write down what qualities, behaviors, and attitudes they want to affirm in each other. The structure of the handout is, each sibling is to note one thing they appreciate in the way the others relate, and another in the way they work. These being the two main ways of improving organizational performance, I wanted them to focus on both relational connectedness and operational proficiency.

When they had finished writing, we sat on chairs in a circle, and I had them say their statements to each other. We started with one person in the spotlight, and the others used their notes to tell that individual what they appreciated. They made statements like:

- ▶ "I can tell that you are all in for me, for our family, and for the organization."
- ▶ "You make it safe for me to be myself, and I never feel judged by you."

▸ "I appreciate that you want a relationship with me outside of work."

▸ "You use your talents and gifts in ways that amaze me."

It was quite a successful experience. I could see that the siblings meant what they said and that they were moved by each other's statements.

When it was over, I said, "Okay, we've just had what's called a process. Now let's process the process. What was this like for you?"

The responses were positive: "I appreciated what they said." "I didn't know they noticed my strengths that much." "I feel like we're more of a team now."

But the comment that stuck with me the most was, "I actually already knew how they felt about me. We're siblings, so we grew up together and we know each other really well, so no real surprises. I didn't think this exercise would mean anything to me, because it wouldn't be new information. But I was surprised by how it felt to hear it from them. It was like I needed to hear it, but I didn't know I needed to hear it, and when I heard it, it met some kind of need inside."

He was exactly right. We need to hear the good from each other. Even if it's something we know another person feels, we still need to hear it. Our brains are wired for relationship, especially in how relationship delivers important emotional information. The cognitive part of our brain can read a list and learn some facts, and that helps. But unless we also engage the experiential part, which involves relationships and emotions, the facts don't become transformational and life-changing.

It's like the story in which one evening a wife, feeling a bit insecure, asked her husband, "Do you love me?" He replied, "I told you I loved you at our wedding thirty years ago. Until you hear anything from me to contradict that, you can assume that statement is still in effect." I'm sure the rest of the evening did not go well for him.

This is especially true in leadership, whether it be in an organization, as a parent, or in some other capacity in which you influence others. Leaders carry around a relational megaphone, whether or not they know it. What I mean by this is that the normal impact we have on others with our words is amplified by the leadership role. That type of relationship causes those we seek to lead to pay more attention to what we tell them. Over and over, I have heard people tell me something a leader told them about themselves that inspired them, encouraged them, and built them up, still motivating them even decades later. So it's important to be aware of what we say, why we say it, and how we say it.

If a reality about someone is good, they need to hear it and we need to say it. If we notice it, we need to hear it and say it. The Bible teaches again and again that words have enormous power. "Gracious words are a honeycomb, sweet to the soul and healing to the bones" (Prov. 16:24).

That passage describes well the nature of the second quadrant of relational nutrients. The six nutrients in this quadrant provide words which dispense grace (sweetness to the soul) and health (healing to the bones), helping others feel more positive about themselves and their lives. You need it for yourself, as do others in your sphere of influence.

AFFIRMATION

A friend of mine was over at my house recently, working on some home improvements. I asked him how his family was, knowing his adult son and his wife had had their first child, a son.

He said, "I wish I weren't surprised, but I actually am surprised at what a great dad he is. His teenage years were not a lot of fun, so I wasn't confident that he'd really grow up to be a good family man. But he is attentive, nurturing, and makes the boy a very high priority."

"That's awesome," I said. "Have you let him know how you feel?"

"Yes, the other day I wrote him an email just telling him how proud I am of him."

"How did he respond?"

"He was blown away. I had no idea how much it would mean to

him. I didn't get any of that from my dad, so I'm sure I didn't do it much with my son. But he was really appreciative of it."

Have you ever been blown away by a random compliment from someone who matters to you? It is simply a gift to us, one that brings positivity, a sense of being an okay person, and a feeling that we matter. Affirmation is noticing a quality in a person, or an achievement of theirs, which required effort on their part. It is bringing attention to something valuable in another's character, and it is often like pouring water on the dry soil of a plant. Our minds drink up the nutrient, and we feel invigorated.

What is more, we then tend to pay more attention to those qualities and work harder to develop them. One person explained it to me this way: "When someone I care about notices something that is true and good about me, it makes me believe it more than I do."

To be a helpful nutrient, affirmation has to be attached to effort. To affirm a quality that a person has put no effort into does little good as a relational nutrient and, when done repeatedly, can even create feelings of insecurity or entitlement. The insecurity is derived from a fear that this is all I have of value, and the entitlement can come from the attitude that I don't have to work for anything and I deserve popularity and appreciation for nothing. "You've got a great smile" and "You're smart" (both gifts that require no work to get) are just not as growth-producing as "You love your friends," "You work really hard," and "You are making the most of your talents."

Also, the more specific an affirmation is, the more power it has. Try to minimize "You're amazing" and "You're special." Those are general and a bit lazy. Instead "You have an amazing ability to see the bigger picture when others are lost in the weeds, and I see you express it to great benefit in our company" is much more helpful.

It's much easier to provide affirmation than to ask for it. We often feel that we are being self-centered if we request that someone affirm a good thing about us. But how do others know we need it if we don't ask for it?

I worked with a business owner who was so concerned about being prideful that, though he had accomplished great things, he never let his wife know how much it would mean for her to affirm what he had done. So she figured it wasn't important to him and that he didn't need it. As a result, when he would mention that he had just acquired another company, she would be interested and ask a few questions but never praise him for what he did. At the same time, another part of him wanted to be seen and known by her, though he was afraid to ask.

I could tell that this was important to him, and we all three talked about it. When I told her how he felt, she said to him, "This is a huge surprise! After all these years of marriage, I have admired you so much, but I just didn't think it was anything you wanted from me. I am so grateful and impressed by all you have accomplished as a husband, dad, and businessperson." Then she ticked off some of the qualities she appreciated.

Tears came to the man's eyes. He drank in her affirmations, and then he said, "I am so sorry I've never been honest about how much I need you to notice what I do. I don't need it all the time, but I'll let you know when I really feel I'd like it."

As you see on the safety warnings at the airport, "If you see it, say it." And let's add to that, "If you need it, ask for it." There is a reason why Jesus mentioned the affirmation of the responsible servant in the parable of the talents. "His master replied, 'Well done, good and faithful servant! You have been faithful with a few things; I will put you in charge of many things. Come and share your master's happiness!'" (Matt. 25:23). It is a model of how we are to speak to one another as well.

Sample: "In your marriage, you two have done a great job navigating how you have grown closer, when you could have easily given up."

ENCOURAGEMENT

It's as simple as this: the cure for discouragement is encouragement. We all become discouraged in life, leadership, and relationships when we have been facing multiple challenges and are beginning to wonder if we have what it takes to overcome them. The root term of both words is an old French word, *encoragier*, which means "to hearten." So we lose heart from time to time, which is discouragement, and the way back is to have someone restore our heart, which is encouragement.

As a relational nutrient, encouragement is built on a deficit, the deficit of discouragement. A person who is walking through life feeling good and confident doesn't need encouragement, but a person whose tank feels empty certainly does. That is what sets encouragement apart from affirmation. You can affirm anyone at just about any time, if it's meaningful and authentic. If they need it at the time, so much the better. If they don't, and it just happens spontaneously, it's like a deposit in a savings account. It's there to draw on when the person needs to remember later what you said.

I was coaching the senior pastor of a large church. The church had gone through financial upheavals and unexpected leadership and staff transitions; there was a great deal of unrest. As senior pastor, my client was the focus of everyone's unhappiness, regardless of what was his fault, and the great majority of the issues were not his fault.

But the criticisms started getting to him, like a dripping faucet that can't be ignored. He began questioning whether he was the right guy for the job. He questioned his capacities and fitness to do the work, a classic profile of discouragement.

During one of our sessions, he mentioned he had heard some more bad news, that the local newspaper was writing an unflattering article about the church's troubles. He was as down as I had ever seen him.

I said, "You are very discouraged, and I understand that with all that's going on, you are feeling a great deal of insecurity and questioning whether you have what it takes to continue leading this church. Probably anybody would. But can you do me a favor? Can you, while your inner judge is saying lots of negative things about your fitness, try to put those thoughts aside and listen to my observations? I promise I'll be as truthful as I know how, and I won't flatter you or blow smoke."

He agreed.

"You haven't been perfect, and you have made some errors as senior pastor," I said. "But the great majority of the decisions I have seen you make, and the ways you have led, have been exemplary. You have the requisite gifts of being a leader. You guard the mission and vision, you guide your people, you inspire, and you train others. When there are problems in the church, you analyze what's going on, bring in others, and act decisively. If you aren't the right guy, I honestly don't know who would be. So what are you feeling when I tell you this?"

"I don't feel great," he said, "but I can feel a shift. The discouragement is lessening. It's as if I am drawing on your belief in me and taking it as my own."

"That makes sense, and that is what should be happening. I want you to write down the main points of what I said and go to your three strongest supporters and ask them to tell you their thoughts about this as well. You will need to review these comments in the next few weeks until things straighten out."

He did that, and he was able to persevere. He is still doing well in that church, and the storms, at least those storms, have passed.

That is the nature of encouragement. You lend your authentic and true belief in the other person until they can own it for themselves and use it independently. And we all need it. "Encourage one another and build each other up, just as in fact you are doing" (1 Thess. 5:11).

Sample: "I am really discouraged about my inability to find the right career direction. I need your encouragement that I truly can do this."

RESPECT

One of the best leadership talks I ever heard was that of a business owner whose team had worked like sled dogs to execute an important initiative which, unfortunately, had not delivered the desired outcomes. They all met to debrief the problem and figure out what happened, understandably discouraged and disappointed in themselves.

The owner took a moment and said, "I know we'll get to the bottom of this, and I want to know my part in the results as well. But I need for you to know that even though we aren't happy with how this ended up, I have had the greatest respect for the perseverance, energy, and commitment you showed in the process. The outcome was something to learn from. But my respect for how you proceeded in this initiative is boundless."

You could feel the positivity creeping back into the executive conference room. They had just been given the right relational nutrient at a time when they most needed it.

Respect is honor or assigned value. When you convey respect to someone, you are expressing to them that they occupy a place of honor in your mind and that you see great value in them or in something about them. "Show proper respect to everyone" (1 Peter 2:17).

We need an infusion of respect at times when we are not sure that we feel respectful of ourselves, as in the case of the business team. We also need it when we wonder if people have a positive view of us, and there is no information in that regard coming toward us.

There are three main things we need respect for and are to provide others respect for.

1. *Character.* It helps us to know that our care for others, hard work, honesty, and vulnerability are noticed and appreciated. "I respect your values and your efforts" goes a long way.
2. *Choices.* There are times when a person makes difficult decisions. When these are recognized and respected, it helps the person feel confident and supported enough to fight another day. "I really respected how you didn't shirk from having the hard talk with your mom last week. That had to be difficult to do."
3. *Freedom to choose.* It is important for our choices to be respected, even those others may not agree with. One of the big takeaways of learning boundaries is that we are to respect the

freedom of others to make their own choices, rather than trying to control their choices. When we embrace that freedom and show respect, we are helping them to own their decisions and learn from the consequences. "I respect that you are choosing to invest in this speculative stock. I may not agree with you, but I respect that you are making your own choices and taking responsibility for them."

HOPE

While encouragement targets your present situation, hope focuses on the future. Hope is the relational nutrient which provides reality-based confidence in a positive outcome down the road. You experience a feeling of assurance that a business move or a relationship challenge will go well as time passes.

I can't overemphasize the value of hopefulness in our lives. When we feel hopeful about the future of our relationships, our health, and our careers, we can persevere even when a positive outcome seems unlikely at the moment. Hope is the energy source which gives us the strength to carry on.

I use the term reality-based confidence because the real and true and usable hope isn't positive thinking or whistling in the dark or hoping against hope. It is founded on something that is actual and exists. "I'm hopeful that your company will grow because I really hope it grows" is useless. That sort of hope is called defensive hope, which Henry Cloud and I describe in our book *Safe People*. It defends us against the discomfort of thinking about what really is involved in creating a good future. Compare that statement with "I'm hopeful that your company will grow because your product fits the market need now, and your new leadership training is helping people to align with your vision." There is substance to this kind of hope. It creates optimism and perseverance to help you do the hard things necessary for success.

In one of my leadership program teams, José, a small business owner in the software industry, came to us concerned about his company's sustainability for the future. He had a history of doing things himself rather than delegating, which kept his business from growing, as no new leadership was being developed. He was also getting behind on his accounts, as he could not keep up with new business. Our team helped him find the courage to delegate and give up micromanaging. However, that meant he had to begin hiring higher-end talent to take over the functions he was handling: finances, operations, marketing, and sales.

When José finally made the right moves, he went into a panic. He was in that very tough transition in business, between spending money for future growth and not seeing the income from it. And he was not likely to see that income for several months. He was losing hope for a truly sustainable business.

One of the team members said to him, "José, I have a lot of hope for your company's future, and I'm not just trying to make you feel better. I have real reasons: You have shown us your P and L statement, and, barring a huge emergency, you have enough cash until the new money comes in. You are investing in the right people for the right positions. You are beginning to lead at a higher level, concentrating on running your company from a mission level, and dealing personally with only the top 10 percent of your clients."

I said, "I agree. You are sowing the right things, and I have great and solid hope that you will reap the right things. It is just how God's process works."

José's face showed less stress as we talked. He said, "I'm seeing a bit of light at the end of the tunnel. You guys are not just being nice to me. You are showing me that what I am doing today should have the right outcomes in the future."

And that is what happened. In a few months, the cash situation eased up, and José began experiencing the hoped-for future that he had worked so hard for.

On a family level, I worked with a couple whose teenage son was acting out, skipping school, and doing drugs. They asked me for help and hope. So I asked them what they were doing about his behavior.

"We try to encourage him and be positive," they said. "We don't think it's helpful to be negative and upset him."

I said, "Unfortunately, I need to tell you that with your current stance toward your son, the situation is hopeless."

They were upset. "Hopeless? We came to you for hope, and this is what you give us?"

"Let me clarify. I said that this is hopeless with your current stance. Your son does need encouraging and positive parents. But he also needs structure, limits, consequences, a good adolescent therapist, and a teen twelve-step group. It would be the same as my telling you that if you choose to eat three bags of chips and four sodas every day and never work out, your desire to be healthy is hopeless. I would like for you to rethink how you want to handle this, and if it's the way I'm suggesting, I have lots of hope."

Fortunately, they got it and reworked their parenting approach. It was still difficult, but now the teen is a young man in his twenties who is doing well.

Hope deferred does make our heart sick (Prov. 13:12). So if you are feeling a bit sick about your personal or professional future, it may be that your hope has been deferred because it's not based on reality. Of course, we can't control all of our circumstances, and bad things happen to good people. But a great deal of the time, meaningful hope can be transferred from one person to another.

If the realities aren't there (for the business or the teen or whatever), then you must be honest, providing hope at a deeper level. "I share your concern that the company might go negative on cash. I will help you strategize ways to find funds to bridge you over, and I have hope that there are appropriate sources out there." "Your son has refused to participate in any of the treatments you have sent him to, and now he's eighteen. So now that he's no longer a minor, we can't hope against hope that he will recover soon. You can offer him help to whatever extent you can afford it when he's ready, stay in some relationship with him, and pray for him."

When you feel somewhat hopeless, ask for the relational nutrient of hope. Give it and receive it as needed, always based on the realities you are aware of.

Sample: "If I thought you wouldn't be able to make the quarterly goals, I would tell you that. But given your new strategy, how you are leading now, and the people you have around you, I have a high confidence level that you'll hit your targets."

FORGIVENESS

If there is such a thing as a default nutrient, it's this one. Forgiveness is one of the most powerful and energizing relational nutrients that exist. I have seen forgiveness heal marriages, families, and even businesses. When in doubt, provide and receive forgiveness.

Forgiveness is the cancellation of a debt. It is saying, "You broke it, but I will repair it." It is saying, "The innocent one pays." Whether the subject is broken trust, a broken heart, or embezzled funds, it means you "[forgive] each other, just as in Christ God forgave you" (Eph. 4:32).

Whether you are providing or receiving this nutrient, you benefit. Receivers as well as givers are better off.

Mark, a client of mine who ran a very successful investment business, had a partner steal more than a million dollars from him. To make matters worse, the partner had been one of his best friends. Mark was understandably devastated by the betrayal.

There are times when people should be accountable to pay the consequences for their behavior. That is what debt repayment, reparations, and prison terms are all about. A bank robber may be truly remorseful, but he still needs to do his time.

There are other times when it is not the best idea to hold the person accountable. That was Mark's case, because the partner had gone bankrupt and was destitute. It would have taken an impossible amount of time to pay Mark back. Mark could have pushed for a long-term repayment, and he would have been legally justified in this, and sometimes this can be the right thing to do.

However, as Mark and I talked about this many times, he made the decision to just cut his losses, write it off, and forgive the debt. I asked him, "Are you sure about this? You could legitimately work on getting a lien against all his future earnings."

He said, "I could, but I need to be free of this guy in my head. Every time I think about chasing him down, being with lawyers and judges on the case, and doing this for years, I get tired. I'm better off letting him go, both financially and emotionally."

The point here is that when we don't forgive, we run the risk of giving control of our lives to the offender. Psychologists talk about how we tend to obsess about that person, dream about what they have done, think about ways they have hurt us, and transfer our negative feelings about that person onto other relationships. Forgiveness wipes the slate clean so we can move on.

Again, just to be clear, Mark could have held his partner to a payment plan. Physically and emotionally abusive spouses need to experience consequences. Criminals need to be incarcerated. But in any of these cases, the offended party is responsible to cancel the emotional debt. "I will not wait for you to repair my damaged emotions. I will handle that myself. You are off the hook for that. I may not trust you, for trust is earned. But I am no longer going to hold this against you." That is freedom.

Forgiveness is not the same as healing. Sometimes people think, *I don't need to talk about this event or this relationship, because I forgave that person.* This is usually not true. It's more because they don't want to feel the depth of their hurt, sadness, and anger about the situation. A better perspective is that forgiveness is a choice and healing is a process. Begin the process of healing by forgiving. That gets you on God's operating table, where he works on you and with you to put your life back together.

On a practical level, then, when you have wronged someone and know you need to apologize and ask for forgiveness, do it. In our current culture, we don't do this very much. It's more commonly said, "My bad, sorry," and the hope is that the other person says, "It's okay, thanks." That's better than nothing, but I would suggest we restore the potency of the word forgiveness.

Here is a bit of a dilemma. Suppose you wrong someone and they refuse to forgive you? Or suppose they have died? This is worse than a dad having to walk down the hall to his kid's bedroom to ask forgiveness. How do you go on in the limbo of being unforgiven?

The solution has several parts to it. First, experience forgiveness from God. "If we confess our sins, he is faithful and just and will forgive us our sins and purify us from all unrighteousness" (1 John 1:9). We all need this form of God's own relational nutrient. Second, let someone who is for you know about it. Just unburden yourself to them, even if you are embarrassed about it. That person can't forgive you, as they are not the offended party. But they can and should provide you with the relational nutrient of acceptance, which will help a great deal. "Yes, you did screw up with her. Yes, you and I are okay. And yes, I'll help you get through this." And third, do whatever you need to do in your own growth and healing to resolve what drove you to do the things you did, so that it doesn't happen again. That is your best case.

Forgiveness solves so many personal and professional issues. Don't do it in your head. Do it in relationship, and you will experience the benefits.

Sample: "What your husband did was wrong, and it damaged you. That is reality. But I want to help you forgive him so you can heal from the damage and move on."

CELEBRATION

Some people are natural celebrators of a win, and some have to work at it a bit. Whichever end of the spectrum you are on, it is worth it to learn how to transfer this nutrient.

Celebration is the acknowledgment of a win, both cognitively and emotionally. It's the pop-the-cork experience which brings everyone into the revelry, whether the occasion is a schoolchild making honor roll, a high school teen being accepted by her dream school, a friend losing thirty pounds, or a business partner landing a multimillion-dollar account. When we celebrate, endorphins are released and "feel good" abounds.

There are three purposes for this nutrient. First, celebration requires that we be in the moment, what psychologists term mindfulness. It is so easy for us, especially those of us who are more get-it-done people, to just move to the next task after a win. Think about a professional sports event in which the team has just won a semifinal game in front of millions of fans who are going crazy. The reporter interviews the head coach, who inevitably says, "We had a good game, and now we need to get ready for next week's game." I always want to say, "C'mon, coach, how many times do your players need to dunk orange Gatorade on your head for you to be happy?" Celebration forces us to experience, in our thoughts and in our feelings, what is going on right now.

Second, celebration is a reinforcer. It increases the likelihood that we will repeat whatever actions we performed to make the party happen. Positive reinforcers help us remember the good, to make the good reoccur.

Third, celebration connects us to each other. Think about the celebrations you have been part of, either yours or someone else's, and how bonded and attached people become to each other. You see this at weddings, baby showers, housewarmings, and retirement parties. A friend of mine called me one day and said, "My wife and I just paid off the mortgage and burned it in the back yard. We're taking you and Barbi to dinner!" We were so thrilled and happy for them.

Let's get back to those who struggle with celebrating. Remember my term narcissism phobia from the introduction to part 2, when I was telling the CEO that he needed to put his wares out into the public better. This is a major cause for not being able to celebrate; instead people say, "Let's go to the next game" or, in the Christian version, "It's not me; it's God." Let me give you an illustration of this from my own life, and the solution as well.

I've always had a great deal of respect and love for my parents, who have passed away. They did a very good job of raising me and my three sisters, and all of their children turned out to be decent people, with the possible exception of their son (I'm kidding).

One day when my father was still alive, I was on the phone with him, and was feeling a good deal of gratitude. So I said, "I just wanted you to know how much I appreciate what a good dad you were in the child-rearing days. Now that I'm a dad, I see how much work it is. You and Mom raised four kids, you took care of your marriage, you paid all the bills and worked long hours to do it, you sent us all through college, and you gave us a Christian foundation. Thank you."

Dad said, "That wasn't me; that was Jesus."

"Well, I know Jesus ran everything, but you put a lot of effort into this as well."

"I don't want to get a big head about this. I just give the credit to Jesus."

I was aware that he was a humble man who also had a touch of narcissism phobia. He didn't want praise to go to his head. At the same time, I wanted him to celebrate being a great dad. So I said, "Here's how I see it. We have two tanks inside us, as if we were a car and these are fuel tanks. One is a pride tank, which we should starve, as pride isn't good for us, right?"

He agreed.

"And the other is an 'I'm celebrating because God used me to do good things' tank. And I think we shouldn't starve that tank; otherwise we miss out on the happiness of being part of his plan."

My father was a rational and scientific man. The phone was silent for about a minute. I had no idea what he would say. Then he said, "You're welcome."

Dad got it. If narcissism phobia makes it hard for you to celebrate, just remember to let the party go to the second tank.

If you tend to get stuck in the "head down, next task" stance, I recommend you use someone in your life who is a natural celebrator as a starter switch. Talk to them about your victory. Watch how excited they get about your win. When we are around their happiness, celebration becomes contagious. As Jesus taught in the parable of the prodigal, sometimes it's the right time to have a party. "Bring the fattened calf and kill it. Let's have a feast and celebrate" (Luke 15:23).

Sample: "I think I crushed it on the Thompson account. Let me take you out!"

WHICH QUADRANT TO USE WHEN?

This is a good time to clarify when you should use a Q1 or Q2 nutrient or which one you need in a particular situation. Quadrant 2 nutrients still require the presence and being there that Q1 nutrients require. But they are more clearly about saying the right things at the right time, with more words involved. I find that it's best, when in doubt, to default to Q1, whether you are the one in need or you are helping someone else. It's less disruptive to have to move up from Q1 to Q2 than to have to reverse course and drop back from Q2 to Q1.

Suppose you have a friend who is struggling in his career and is unloading his unhappiness with you. You start with a Q2 statement, such as "You have so many strengths; I believe in you." That's often a good thing to say. But if he's really discouraged, he is likely to feel, *I really don't need a pep talk. I need you to just be in my world.* Better to begin with presence and then move to words.

Well-chosen words can bring life to you, and your words can bring life to others. Be aware of which of the six Q2 nutrients you need in any given situation. As you practice this, you will know much more competently what others need as well.

One small caveat: even though Q2 involves more words than Q1 does, don't overdo the total word count. Sometimes we think people need every detail of all the affirmations and encouragements we think of for them. We go on and on, with good intentions in our heart. But sometimes it's too much, and that's often because we, in some perfectionistic way, are trying to make sure we give them every bit of what they need.

If you tend toward this, back off a tad and trust that a few statements and one example are probably enough. When I was working on my doctorate in psychology, one of my mentors and professors, Dr. Bruce Narramore, was lecturing about how much a psychologist should talk with a client in session. He said, "Some therapists think they need to bathe the client in words, but I think we risk drowning them." Just use the right words. As Proverbs 10:19 says, "When there are many words, transgression is unavoidable, but he who restrains his lips is wise" (NASB).

CHAPTER 9

QUADRANT 3

Provide Reality

"I HAVE USABLE INFO"

I'll never forget the day I had to be a total downer to a young, excited, passionate startup company. They were in the software arena; I had been consulting with their executive team about how they were going to drive their innovations and scale. The emotions were contagious. The team had a product with lots of promise, they were creative, and they cared.

The hiccup was that I had been reviewing their financials before the team meeting. The numbers were scary. They were in over their heads in cost overruns, and they were in a cash crunch. More than that, I had been following their projections of great sales, based on innovative ideas, for several months, and the sales were not even close to projections.

They started the meeting with the vision and the passion. Marketing and sales led the charge. Then, when Will, the CFO, began to bring out the negative realities, they were irritated and said that he didn't believe in the vision and was too risk averse. But the numbers were the numbers, and I knew Will enough to believe that this was not just some risk-aversion problem. His concerns were credible.

Usually I am very much a win-win person, but in this instance I felt I had to be clear and direct. I stepped in and said, "He's right and you guys are wrong." Not a real consultant-like way to talk, but I was concerned and a bit alarmed, and I wanted to drive home a reality. "I've been over the numbers and have been tracking things for a while. Your company has so many things going for it, and I do have hope that you will be the next big thing. But you are ignoring some very important facts, and the facts are that your burn rate is unsustainable and your sales projections are not coming anywhere close to reality. You will be in serious trouble if you don't listen to your CFO's facts and change course dramatically very soon."

Talk about a buzzkill. The energy and passion drained out of the room. Except the CFO seemed to brighten up a bit. I didn't say anything more. I was waiting to see what the CEO would do with my response, as I felt that what she said next would make all the difference.

I was relieved and pleased when she said, "I have been hoping that the initiatives and projections would change the financial picture, but that has not happened, and I don't think we can wait any longer to do something. I need for us to talk about rethinking our product line, marketing, and sales and to work together as a team to bring us into financial reality. We have a lot of talent here, and I am confident that we can make the changes we need to make. I don't want to squelch the passion at all. But Will, I need you to have the floor here, and we need to pay attention to the concerns you have. Our changes will have to exist within your parameters."

Within a few months, the company had made some hard decisions, but they got on the right track. They also preserved the positive energy the team needed. The moral of this story is that any successful endeavor must be oriented to and welcome truth. This includes marriage, dating, parenting, friendship, careers, and leadership. People who do well in life seek out the truth and orient to whatever it says, rather than cherry-picking the truths that fit their idea.

Truth is simply what is. If something is true, it corresponds to reality and is not based on perceptions or distortions. It can be trusted, and we can make weighty decisions based on it. We are to value it greatly. "Buy the truth and do not sell it" (Prov. 23:23). We grow, prosper, and heal through understanding and applying truths that make a difference.

My workout trainer is a research fanatic, and every time we get together, he shares the latest nutrition and musculoskeletal findings he has come across, and he adjusts my program to fit the newly discovered truths (even though he has a particularly noncompliant client to work with). The truths guide the process.

Also, as I mentioned before, truth is available to us in many forms (biblical principles, research, logic, intuition, feedback). Truth is also a relational nutrient, occupying its own category (Q3: Provide Reality). If we want to make a difference, we should be seeking out truth for ourselves and providing it for others in ways that are useful. In this chapter, there are five nutrients that have to do with truth. You will see how helpful the right kind of truth, in the right relational setting, can be for yourself and others.

"These are the things you are to do: Speak the truth to each other, and render true and sound judgment in your courts" (Zech. 8:16). The inference here is clear: the more truth transferred, the better life goes.

CLARIFICATION

Some truths—a new idea, a new piece of data—come from outside us. However, some truths come from simply getting rid of the static in our brains; the answer was there all along. This second situation is what clarification is all about. I define clarification as helping a person think clearly enough to see an answer. This is not about the thinking that says, "Seek within you; all the answers are there." That makes no sense, and many people have suffered from seeking within instead of seeking God or wise people. But sometimes we do have an answer that we simply didn't have clarity on, and that is where clarification can be very helpful.

I began working with a man who owned a multigenerational family business in the transportation industry. He told me up front, "I'm done. I think I want to sell it."

I was curious and said, "Let me know more about that. It's certainly a huge decision for you."

We talked about his company, and his relationship with his company, over a series of conversations. I knew this was not a time to give advice or guidance, because I just didn't have enough facts to come even close to providing those. So I asked a great deal of clarifying questions. A clarifying question is focused on eliminating confusion. Here is a brief overview of the conversations I had with my client, involving these kinds of questions and showing how each succeeding question was based on what I learned from the former one.

"Why do you think you want to sell the business?"

"I used to love it, and it's making a good profit, but I can't stand working there anymore."

"What can you not stand?"

"I don't like walking into the office in the morning."

"What do you not like about walking into the office?"

"It's all about solving problems and having meetings."

"And that's not what you want?"

"It's not the way it was."

"How did it used to be?"

"I did deals. I love the thrill of the hunt and negotiating great deals."

"So solving problems and having meetings isn't who you are?"

"Absolutely not. I don't like being tied to a desk and going to meetings. I feel trapped and I hate it."

"Yet the company needs those functions. What if someone else did those and reported to you, and you were freed up to do the hunt?"

"I'd like that, but I haven't found anyone who can do a good enough job so that I can trust them."

"Have you looked for those types?"

"Not really, because to afford to do that, I'd have to let go of some people who don't do a great job, but they've been here a long time, and I'd feel bad about letting them go."

"If we could find a way so that you didn't feel so bad, would that be a direction you'd want to go?"

"Maybe."

Long story short, he dealt with the guilt he felt, by working through some codependency issues he had. That freed him up to prune back the nonperformers and hire some performers. And by the time this was all done, he was back in love with the business.

You'll notice that in this series of questions, the only new truth I provided was the idea of working through his bad feelings. The rest was just probing to get to what he needed to see for himself.

That is the nature and value of clarification. It just clears up the mud in the water. Jesus used this nutrient too. "As Jesus started on his way, a man ran up to him and fell on his knees before him. 'Good teacher,' he asked, 'what must I do to inherit eternal life?' 'Why do you call me good?' Jesus answered. 'No one is good—except God alone" (Mark 10:17–18). Jesus was clarifying his authority. In essence, he told the man, "You are saying I am good, so you are agreeing that I am God." It is a powerful way of helping with truth, because people have to work on it themselves rather than reading a list of principles.

Have you ever had a life challenge and just wanted to unpack it with someone who knew how to clarify, versus someone who would give you advice as soon as you started your story? Our brain wants and needs to think about matters itself; we just need some help. The best decisions I have made in my life were based on probably 80 percent clarification from the right people and 20 percent advice.

The well-known Toyoda Five Whys[2] is a great example of clarification. With this system, the person moves from the symptom of the problem to its root and a solution, most of the time within five iterations of the right why.

And with personal issues, clarification helps a great deal. A teenager who is thinking about dropping a class he doesn't like won't listen if you tell him what he has to do, but he will benefit from this nutrient: "Let's talk about what happens to your privileges if you drop the class, and what happens if you stick with it." Clarification keeps the focus on what options the teen needs to consider, rather than on a fight with authority.

Unless you are in an urgent situation or have very little time with someone, start with clarification if there is a question of truth. You may not have to move to any other type of information delivery. And if you do, you and the person will be much more zeroed in on the specific type of information that will be most useful.

Sample: "Why do you think you put up with your daughter's disrespect so much? There has to be a reason for this."

PERSPECTIVE

Yesterday I was training leaders at a workshop, and a woman who runs a small business asked me for some help in dealing with a personal issue, which had to do with her relationship with her mother. She said her mom was highly dependent on her, and if she did not talk to her mom every day and visit often, her mom would become sad and lonely and complain to her that she wasn't looking after her. Her mom resisted making friends, so this woman was her only source of life.

We discussed all this, and I did a role play with her, in which she played the mom and I played the "healthy her." I set it up so that Mom and I were having a visit, and I was to introduce the topic. So I said, "Hi, Mom. How have you been? I need to talk about something that's important to me, and that is our relationship. I'd like to improve how we communicate and can be closer." Then we went into the issue itself, which basically revolved around being kind but less available and helping Mom to find some good friends.

After the exercise, the woman said to me, "That was helpful, but at the same time, it felt like my mom was being blindsided. She didn't expect this kind of conversation, because usually we talk about her health and her personal problems. Is this really the right approach?"

I said, "Well, we never want to be harsh or mean. But what you call blindsiding someone, I think would more accurately be called changing the conversation to a different area of importance. Maybe that would be a surprise to her, but I don't see it as a bad thing."

Since the woman was a Christian, I offered a biblical example. "Let's take the story of David and Nathan, when Nathan told him a story about a rich man who stole a lamb from a poor man. David was incensed and wanted to bring justice to the rich man. Then Nathan said, 'You are the man!' (2 Sam. 12:7), because it was really about David's affair with Bathsheba. So was David blindsided?"

"Yes," the woman said. "But I can see that the approach helped him to see his actions in a new way."

"Exactly. Nathan gave David another perspective, a better and truer way to look at what he had done. And it changed David's life. So today, you and I are providing two new perspectives at once. First, I am giving you a new perspective on how to improve your relationship with your mom. And second, hopefully, you will give her a new perspective on how to relate to you and deal with her unhappiness."

And that's all perspective is. It is to offer someone a different and more helpful way to view a situation, another lens to use.

None of us sees every reality about ourselves. We all have blind spots, both positive and negative. We don't see how loving and kind we are, and we don't see how disconnected and self-absorbed we are. We truly don't know what we don't know. And this not knowing extends beyond ourselves to the people, family members, and organizations with which we engage.

When someone gives you a fresh look at yourself, it is an aha moment, when the lights come on and you feel more clarity about who you are and why you have done what you have done. When you do the same for another, often that person has the same experience.

When you are challenged with a personal or professional situation, just ask someone for this nutrient, saying, "I need perspective, because I'm not sure whether I'm seeing it all the right way." It can change the entire way you operate.

Sample: "It seems that with your daughter, you are more focused on controlling her behavior than you are on helping her grow up and learn from her choices."

INSIGHT

I was having dinner with Beth and Troy, a couple whom I knew well, and the conversation moved to their relationship. It was a solid marriage in the main. They weren't having major struggles, but minor struggles are still struggles. So I asked for each of them to say what things are like, from their own vantage point.

Beth went first. "I really love Troy, and he's never unkind to me. But he's often distant and remote. It's like I just want him to connect and for us to enter each other's emotional worlds. But if I don't push it, it doesn't happen, and most of the time not even then."

"Got it," I said. Then I turned to Troy.

He said, "I love Beth, and she's the best thing that's ever happened to me. But sometimes I feel that I can never connect enough. I want to be there emotionally with her. But I don't do it right or say the right things or do it long enough or take enough initiative. So I'm sure I do check out."

After hearing this, I said, "You both have issues."

They started laughing, and said, "Oh, that was so insightful."

"But I think you aren't aware of the true issues." To Beth, I said, "You came from a family in which your mom was preoccupied with her job, her health, and your siblings. When she was present with you, she did a good job. But it was inconsistent and not a steady flow of attunement. It created in you a fear of being abandoned. I think Troy has a point, that there may be a 'never enough' inside you that is real, and that is an issue you want to focus on for growth."

I told Troy, "You came from a workaholic family that worked and worked and worked. Emotional, relational conversations were not in the family DNA. So here comes Beth with a need to connect, and part of you feels overwhelmed and incompetent. So you will need to develop your connection muscle more.

"So the bottom line is that you, Beth, are afraid of being alone, and you, Troy, are afraid of being overwhelmed by her needs. You both have work to do!"

They looked at each other, and Beth smiled slightly. "He's right," she said. "We're both afraid. But I don't want to overwhelm you."

The lights were going on for Troy too. "I don't want you to feel alone."

I knew they would be fine after that, and indeed they were. And they still are.

Insight is making sense of the real issue of a situation. It's getting to the core of a problem or dilemma. People who are reflective and thoughtful are great dispensers of insight.

Beth and Troy got the insight which gave them clarity on what was really going on. Insight is that deeper look into what is causing a problem. Here are some examples.

- ▶ A COO figures out that a low-productivity quarter resulted not from a lack of motivation and work ethic but from her employees' lack of engagement in their jobs.
- ▶ A doctor finds that a fever and chills is caused not by a virus but by a bacterial infection.
- ▶ An executive pastor determines that low attendance is caused by a lack of a sense of community between Sunday services.
- ▶ A CFO determines that a cash issue is caused by overaggressive investments in risky ventures.
- ▶ A dad discovers that his teenage son's withdrawal and crankiness is caused by smoking pot and depression.

Jesus modeled insight in many ways that are lessons to us as well. One of the most significant examples is the story of the woman at the well. He deepens her understanding of her needs, from the physical to the spiritual. "Jesus answered, 'Everyone who drinks this water will be thirsty again, but whoever drinks the water I give them will never thirst. Indeed, the water I give them will become in them a spring of water welling up to eternal life'" (John 4:13–14).

I can never read this passage without feeling the insight Jesus has into my own life, and the hope he provides for all of us. And that is what insight produces. People see beyond their difficulties and are no longer confused or overwhelmed. They see answers, bottom lines, and the real issues. What a helpful nutrient for our personal and professional growth!

Just to clarify here, there is a difference between attunement (Q1) and insight, though there are some similarities. While attunement's focus is entering the other person's experience and ensuring that the individual knows that you are there with them, insight is more focused on comprehending the situation itself. Attunement is about perception and emotion. Insight is about the realities underneath the emotions.

Whenever you are stuck, confused, overwhelmed, or frustrated, do not pass Go. Travel straight to someone who has insight and lay out your experience. It can change your life.

Sample: "It may have been that your sales department struggled because you didn't let the manager go, because of how much you hate conflict."

FEEDBACK

It is as simple as this: feedback is the surgery that successful people constantly seek out. Healthy, helpful feedback provides answers, course correction, and improvements in our organizations, in our families, and in our heads.

I see this "seeking out the surgery" in the highly successful individuals I work with and have relationships with. They don't cringe, they don't avoid it, and they don't dismiss it. They do just the opposite. They ask for it, they appreciate it, and they use it to make things better in their spheres of influence.

Feedback is providing a personal and individualized response to another, to help them in their situation. It can be positive or negative, and it always needs to be delivered from a position of "I'm for you." Research indicates that the most effective feedback is given with more positives and fewer negatives. People need to hear the good to be able to metabolize the challenges.

I was working with the CEO of a large privately held company, who was concerned that his executive team was not gelling. They all tended to relate more to him than to each other. They were always running ideas by him and asking for his insight. But there was very little teamwork among the members themselves. I call this the bicycle wheel model (spokes relating only to the hub), which needs to change to the spiderweb model (all parts relating to all other parts, with the spider still in the center).

I said, "I have been in several team meetings with you chairing, and I think I know what might be a big part of this. You are very strong in your mission clarity, your passion, and the strategy the company is executing. But you talk too much, and that contributes to the lack of team ethos."

Ouch. I wasn't having fun with this part.

He said, "What do you mean?"

"Teams gel when members talk to each other as a team. They need to experience each other's points of view, strengths, passions, and differences. Look at military and sports teams. They are back and forth with each other. But when the leader dominates the meeting, the team has no space to develop trust and cohesiveness. They have tons of trust and cohesiveness with you, but there is not a lot of bandwidth in your meetings for them to develop it with each other."

He was quick to say, "I've never really thought about this, but I think you may be right. My wife has mentioned it a time or two."

"So you have more than one consistent and trustable feedback source. That's good."

"Why do I do that, do you think?"

I always appreciate a leader who asks, "Why?" before he asks,

"What do I do next?" He was after a real understanding before he came to a real solution.

"I think it's a couple of things. First, you're just very excited about the company's direction, and you take off with your passion without being aware that others need to interact more. So just make the passion about 'we' and not 'I,' and that will help. Second, it seems to me that you don't trust them enough to know what to do, so you overtalk it to compensate. You have some real rock stars here, who are better than you are in their area of expertise. Trust them to know what's needed. Then you will tend to talk less and invite their engagement more."

He got it and went right to work on his verbal style. It took a bit of coaching, but his pattern changed dramatically for the better. He gets it still. Things went very well after that, and the team members were catalyzed to become true comrades in arms.

Observe this man's attitude when I intervened on him. No one wants to hear that they talk too much. I have had people walk out of a room in shame and pain when it's been said. It's pretty personal. But this guy had no ego at stake. He was curious about what I meant. He confirmed that someone else had given him similar feedback. He wanted to understand the roots of the problem. And once he understood the cause, he went to work on the solution and changed his behavior.

That is how it should be done, if you are receiving feedback. As David says, "Let a righteous man strike me—that is a kindness; let him rebuke me—that is oil on my head" (Ps. 141:5). When someone is trying to help you and strikes you with some tough feedback, it may be saving your company, your marriage, or your soul.

I have listed and ranked the possible feedback choices.

▶ Positive feedback plus corrective feedback, given warmly
▶ Corrective feedback given harshly
▶ Positive feedback given warmly, with no corrective feedback
▶ No feedback

As you can see, while I much prefer positive feedback plus corrective feedback, given warmly, if I don't have that option, I would rather experience harsh corrective feedback than all positives with no correction. This is because if the person has low EQ and an awful bedside manner and is rude and judgmental, at least I can use the intel from the feedback. Then I can call a friend and vent, and they will make me feel better! That is superior to getting nothing but praise (which, I assure you, never happens to me anyway).

Sample: "If I were your employee, I would think I was human capital to you but not a human. It's hard to be motivated to excel for you. I'd like us to work on changing that."

CONFRONTATION

Confrontation is facing another person with a reality alongside an appeal and warning to change. Sometimes the only and best option in a situation is a confrontation, and it can be healing and transformative. We confront for all sorts of reasons.

- ▶ A direct who is not performing at an acceptable level
- ▶ A teen who is defiant and rude
- ▶ A colleague who is not operating as a team player
- ▶ A spouse who is spending at unhealthy levels
- ▶ A boss who is not providing role clarity and resources for the task
- ▶ A dating relationship in which the person is emotionally unavailable
- ▶ A friend who needs to set better boundaries with her kids

The appeal aspect is that we just want the person to know we are concerned and worried about them, that our motivation comes from love. The warning aspect is that we see that if things don't change, the person will have a negative outcome in their life, and we don't want that. But it all comes from a desire to help and not to punish or judge.

Confrontation and feedback have similarities, but they have two important differences. First, feedback can be an affirmation and positive, or it can be a challenge and a negative. Confrontation, however, is always corrective. You don't say something like, "I confronted her by complimenting her," unless, I suppose, you are confronting her inability to receive praise.

Second, while successful people constantly seek out feedback, it's unusual to seek out confrontation. Most of the time, confrontation is driven by the person wanting to confront, not the confrontee. I've asked for feedback hundreds of times, but I have never asked for confrontation. If I get the first, I always get plenty of the second anyway.

I had lunch with Heather, a friend of my wife and mine. We had not seen each other for a while and were catching up. She was divorced and, after a period of recuperation, was now back in the dating world. She said that she'd had a couple of dates with a nice guy and was hopeful that it could turn into something serious. As she talked about the relationship, she mentioned that she wanted to have him over for dinner to meet her kids. She thought it would be a good introduction all around.

"I need to address this," I said. "Are you okay if I tell you what I think here?"

Heather said, "You have that look on your face. You don't think this is a good idea, do you?"

"No, and because I care about you and your kids, I need to tell you why."

Heather agreed.

"You really handled your kids well during the divorce," I said. "It has been hard on them, but you put in the time and they will be okay. But you have young kids. While your ex is doing a good job being involved, younger kids are more impacted by a new romantic relationship. They attach pretty quickly, because they want an intact family. If you bring this person into their lives, and you haven't been with him long enough to really know each other and to have objective reasons it is highly probable that this will be a long-term relationship, what happens if you two break up in a few months? Then your kids have a second relational loss, and it could be really damaging for them."

She was quiet, and I felt awful. I didn't want to hurt her feelings, as she is a good friend and I really do care about her kids. Long story short, we had a series of conversations about this, and she ended up not introducing him. When the relationship did ultimately end, Heather was sad but knew she had protected her children.

Your life and career can be saved if you hear and respond to the right confrontation. And you could save the life and career of another. I have seen this happen hundreds of times.

The word confront gets a bad valence. We feel anxious about being judged or hurt or being perceived as judgmental or hurtful. But the word is very helpful and positive. As Henry Cloud and I say in our book *How to Have That Difficult Conversation*, "Both the Bible and research show that confrontation is essential to success in all arenas of life. Successful people confront well. They make it a part of the ongoing texture of their relationships. They face issues in their relationships directly. In fact, the Latin word for confront means just that: to turn your face toward something or someone."[3]

Let's face it, being confronted is a very different experience than having someone be present with you (Q1) or encourage you (Q2). Even though it is to be done in an "I'm for you" manner, it usually isn't pleasant, for the confronter or the confrontee. You may wake up in the morning thinking, *I'm looking forward to encouraging Mike in his job performance today.* But if you wake up thinking, *I can't wait to confront Mike on his job performance today*, you have a psychological problem called being a mean person! Nobody should desire to confront. We do it, and we receive it, because it leads to better decisions.

Confrontation can go wrong. Someone can be inaccurate and blame you for something you didn't do. Or they can be harsh and judging of you. Or you can just be in a funk anyway, and it puts you into a deeper funk. Plus, many people have experienced relationships from childhood to adulthood in which they endured a pattern of unhealthy confrontation and have been pretty beat up when they anticipate a tough conversation. And then there are those individuals who had families who never confronted at all, so they have few skills to deal with it and often feel blindsided by it.

Because of these complicating factors, here are a few tips so that the transfer of this relational nutrient will go well.

If you are the confronter:

▸ Convey at the outset that you are for the person.
▸ Think about how you would feel in their shoes and treat them accordingly.
▸ Be soft on the person and hard on the issue.
▸ Make what you want them to change something specific and doable.

If you are the confrontee:

▸ If the person is authentically for you, appreciate their motive.
▸ Be as open and undefensive as possible.
▸ Determine whether their confrontation is accurate and true.
▸ If it's true, act on it.

God intended healthy confrontation to help us be the best person possible. "An honest answer is like a kiss on the lips" (Prov. 24:26). People have told me, years after the fact, that a tough talk I had with them changed their lives for the better. I have experienced that in my own life as well.

Sample: "I'm worried you are neglecting the big picture of your organization by getting distracted by the details. I am concerned that if that continues, your business will suffer significantly."

CHAPTER 10

QUADRANT 4

Call to Action

"I'M MOVING FORWARD"

A client of mine was a wizard at great meetings. Not only were the meetings motivating and clear, but things happened after they ended—the right things. I have been to so many "meetings about meetings," with no real return on the time spent, that I loved going to his.

He told me once, "It's pretty simple for me. I end every meeting with everyone having just one action step."

"That's a low number," I said.

"It is," he replied, "but I have found that we'll have 25 percent follow-up when people have three or four steps, and 90 percent when they have one. It's a matter of focus."

Here is the point. Whether in your professional or your personal life, actions must be part of how you change and grow. We all need the presence of Q1, the positivity of Q2, and the truth of Q3. But the outcome, where the rubber meets the road, must express itself in behaviors of some sort. Doing is important. "Do not merely listen to the word, and so deceive yourselves. Do what it says" (James 1:22).

That's why the fourth quadrant is Call to Action. Great leaders, spouses, parents, and friends all make some sort of appeal to those they are influencing, toward a move, a change, an executable which can get someone moving in the right direction.

Psychologists use the word agency to describe a person's capacity to take initiative and make choices in their lives. Individuals with high agency feel more self-control and competence, while those with lower agency often feel more helpless and overwhelmed. Basically, engaging in a behavior to achieve something you desire creates a positive feeling, whether it be crafting a business strategy, working out in the gym, or driving to a great restaurant for a celebration. With some exceptions, a bad decision is better than no decision. At least there is movement.

A call to action, like Q3's provision of reality, is more about truth than it is about grace, even though it must be delivered with support and love. It's about making a change that needs to be made. Calling someone to action is distinct from providing reality in that sometimes, delivering truth will lead to insight or reflection, what I call the aha moment, when a person's mental paradigm begins to shift. But though a change of behavior might happen, it's not the immediate goal. With a call to action, someone is suggesting to another that they do something meaningful, and soon.

Here is an example of the distinction. I once told a client that he was as rough on his employees as his harsh dad had been on him, an example of insight (Q3). A few months later, he told me that that statement had caused the tumblers to fall into place in his head. Without knowing it, he had done to others what had been done to him. This was because he had idealized his dad and was afraid to deal with the man's flaws and selfishness. As a result of my insight, he faced how his dad really had been and worked through his feelings, experiencing a great amount of healing and forgiveness, which naturally led to his becoming a better boss. He internalized the relational nutrient and did great things with it.

I had just wanted him to be aware of what he was doing, because I knew he was a bulldog who would not let it go, and ultimately he would make some sort of action plan. However, I could have said, "I recommend that for the next sixty days, you concentrate on treating people respectfully and kindly, keeping in mind that this is how you wish your dad had treated you"—a clear action step. That would have been a Q4 nutrient. But I didn't think we had an urgent situation, and I wanted to see if he would take the ball and run with it, which he did. You have to make judgment calls about truth versus action, depending on the situation.

When you call others to action, or when they call you to action, it can be disruptive and uncomfortable. But nobody ever said growth and change were about comfort. It takes energy to transition from inertia to movement. Learn to use the relational nutrients in this quadrant in a way that preserves the relationship but pushes the person toward making a change. There are five you need to have available for yourself and to provide for others.

ADVICE

I have a methodology for coaching busy people that I have termed LaserCOACH. With this approach, I call the individual, go through a structured set of questions with them about their situation, and craft a solution that ends with an action step. It's called laser because it's focused and quick, around fifteen minutes or so. It tends to get highly successful results.

One of the keys of LaserCOACH is that we never end the session without a homework assignment, which is another word for advice, but a specific piece of advice. Then I ask the client to contact my office in a week, and I wait to see what happens, once they are doing what we agreed they would do.

On one call, the client, an executive, was struggling with being late to work meetings and was getting into a bit of hot water with his boss and his team about it. After working through the issues, I gave him one practical piece of advice. Since we had found out that he had people-pleasing tendencies, I knew he had a hard time leaving a meeting in time to attend another one, for fear of letting the first group down. So his assignment was simply to tell people up front, at the beginning of a meeting, that he had a hard stop at, say, 3:30, and if things needed to go later, he would circle back and talk to them. Of course, no one wanted a circle back, because it would take too much planning, so they got things done by 3:30, and he was on his way.

It changed everything for him. He had a structure to rely on, and he got some good practice in telling people his boundaries, which was the internal problem he faced.

That's really all advice is. It's simply recommending a course of action. Advice can be about work, relationships, parenting, or self-care. But the right advice at the right time can be a very effective nutrient. "For lack of guidance a nation falls, but victory is won through many advisers" (Prov. 11:14).

Two things to remember with advice:

1. Determine whether the person needs attunement before your advice. As we see with the well illustration, people get irritated or just ignore advice when it's clear that the adviser is not understanding the personal experience of the advisee. I was talking to a client couple recently, and the wife told her husband, "When we are working on some problem, I need you to stop saying, 'I hear you, but XYZ.'"

He asked, "What do you mean?"

I said, "I think she means instead of saying you hear her, prove to her that you hear her. For example: 'I see that you're overwhelmed and frustrated with the kids, and that makes it hard to want to go out with our friends tonight.'"

She nodded. "Yes, what he said."

We don't always need to attune before advice. When I ask an adviser about some business strategy I'm working on, I just want what he has. Or when I am talking to a friend about a parenting issue, he may say, "I know you get me, John. I just need some pointers." So ask yourself and the person you are trying to help if attunement is needed first.

2. Get permission first. Most of us hate unasked-for advice. It feels parental and patronizing. If a person isn't asking you for advice, but you see some glaring problem that you'd like to help them with, just do what my military friends do and ask for PTSF: permission to speak freely. Then the person has a choice. If it's a truly urgent situation, you may need to forge ahead regardless, as in a drug addiction intervention. But by and large, advice that is permitted is more welcome and more useful.

Sample: "I'd like to suggest that you do a survey to find out exactly how engaged your people are in their positions."

STRUCTURE

A third-generation family-owned business in the financial services industry hired me to work with them. They had been steadily profitable through the years, but the last few had been challenging. Sales and profits were down.

After interviewing the owners and their key players, I realized that they had been successful primarily because they had good products, worked hard, and were competent in relationships. But there was very little sense of organizational structure, in terms of how the pieces all fit. They had not begun that way with Granddad, and things had worked fine. However, with changes such as a global economy, the internet, and shifting cultures, they found themselves behind their competition and were concerned.

So I began my work with the owners by taking them through a presentation of my model of how organizations work. It's called the Funnel. It is literally a graphic of a funnel, and it starts at the top, moving down from the larger view to the smaller focus, in this order: mission, vision, values, culture, goals, strategy, tactics, and vital behaviors. Any organization, large or small, for profit or nonprofit, can prioritize their resources and decisions using this.

I usually get a positive response when I make this presentation, but I was surprised at the level of excitement about the material. In fact, it was not just excitement. It was relief. One of the owners said, "This is our missing piece. We have always done right by people, but we have never had this to organize what we do and to make what we do align to our mission."

I had not realized how big a deal this was, though I probably should have. So we pivoted our focus to the fundamentals: crafting the mission, developing a vision, setting our core values. Though these were fundamentals to lots of organizations, they had not been fundamental to this company. We worked for a year on developing and executing the Funnel, and their results were significantly north of where they had been. The structure focused their energies, people, and decisions.

To structure is to help another by creating a framework to accomplish something. We all need structure for just about anything important to us.

▶ Setting out homework, chores, meals, playtime, and family time for your kids for after school
▶ Crafting a strategic marketing plan
▶ Creating a family calendar of events
▶ Engaging in a workout regimen
▶ Having team meetings to foster healthy culture
▶ Making a budget for the home

Structure involves aspects such as values, priorities, focus, and direction. Relationships are what life is about, but structure orders life so that it works. Without structure, things become chaotic, and important tasks don't get done. "Everything should be done in a fitting and orderly way" (1 Cor. 14:40).

Some people have a great deal of structure already built into their minds. They think in terms of values, priorities, and effectiveness. They tend to be pretty organized. Some are so organized that they spend more time than necessary checking and rechecking the locks at their home or keeping their computer files in perfect order. And some are more comfortable with structure than they are with the messiness of relationships, making connections difficult for them.

Then others have too little structure, for a number of reasons. They have a hard time with impulse control, can be distractible, or have weak boundaries that keep them from staying focused on what is important and needed. What happens when a person with too much rigid structure meets a person without enough structure? They get married!

But the right amount of structure will make just about any issue better. Neuroscience shows us that the brain craves structure. When we have no plans or paths in our lives, the disorder puts us into the amygdala, where flight, fight, freeze, or fold rules us. Structure calms us down, moves us back into the prefrontal cortex, and helps us make great decisions. I have seen many times that when an organization has a 911 situation, and I simply say, "I have a plan for this," people calm down and begin focusing in a more positive way.

That is why it can be very profitable for you to ask for the structure nutrient when you have an issue. Once I provided a couple with a structure for what to do when they got home from work, to help them stay connected. They were out of control with work, kids, and other activities. Part of the plan was that when they got home, instead of jumping right into cooking dinner and getting homework done, they were to give the kids something to do for twenty minutes and just talk to each other about how their day had gone. The structure became a habit which fostered positive feelings, trust, and connection. They stick to it to this day.

So if you need a plan, ask someone who is good with structure to help you craft it. Structure is action-oriented and will help you add order to, and reduce chaos in, your life and leadership.

One caveat: remember that in the main, go to Q1 first, before you go to a plan. Most of the time, attuning, validating, and accepting need to happen before you put together the nuts and bolts of a plan.

Sample: "I'd suggest you set up a strategic offsite with your team, to get things catalyzed and moving in the right direction."

CHALLENGE

Challenge is basically advice with an amplifier. It's more intense and urgent and is needed when someone must pay attention to the next necessary steps. A clear definition is that challenge is strongly recommending an action step, especially a difficult one.

Often we challenge when advice is not working. We escalate what we are saying, taking it to another level. I have a good friend who was ignoring his self-care and scaring his family. He was working too many hours, eating junk, not working out, and spending his weekends catching up on email instead of being with his loved ones. The physical indicators were all there: high blood pressure, cholesterol and glucose, plus weight gain. And so were the emotional indicators: lack of energy, irritability, and shutting down from vulnerable relationships.

When I noticed some of the signs, I mentioned them to him and asked if he was open to advice. He's a truly nice guy, so he agreed. I just mentioned what I had seen, and I suggested he get into a program or hire a coach. He smiled and thanked me. A month later, his wife told me he had appreciated my input. And he had done zero about it. That's when she told me how afraid she was, that he wasn't listening to her, and that she felt helpless, and she asked me for help.

So we had another lunch. It was different in its intent and tone. I expressed to him how important he is to me. Then I said, "I am scared for you. You have some serious indicators that you could have major health problems, and not too far away."

He said, "Thanks for the input. You are totally right. I just have one more big deal to finish up on, and—"

"Stop it. Just stop it," I said. "We've known each other a long time, and I have heard this several times from you. I don't believe you."

He was hurt and said so.

"I'm sorry," I said. "I don't intend to alienate you. But you are closed off from truly listening to me or anyone. You are the most loving and nice family guy in the world. But you aren't taking in what people say. If you were, you would do something about your health."

"I don't think you understand the situation."

"I'm sure you're right; there is a lot I don't understand. Do you believe that I fundamentally respect the fact that you have a very difficult and complicated job? I think I've earned it, because I've been very supportive about this in our conversations over the past few months."

"Yes, you have."

"If that is true, I need for you to listen to how helpless the people you love the most feel around you. Something else must drive you to be as self-sabotaging as you are, because I don't think you love working as much as you do."

"No, I don't."

"Then I really need you to be accountable to your wife and to me, to do three things."

"What are they?"

"The first is to get an appointment with your primary physician ASAP and ask her recommendations for lifestyle change and medications. The second is to get to the gym this week and get a trainer. And if you don't get these two done, you need to go to a counselor I know who works with executives on this sort of problem, because you will need to address your stuckness."

"That's a lot. I'll be out of the weeds with this deal in a month."

I looked at him and said, "I feel absolutely helpless right now. I'll back off. I need to tell your wife about our conversation. I'm sorry. I don't know what else to do."

He froze and looked into space for about thirty seconds. Then he said, "I don't think I can keep ignoring you and her. This is just hell for me, but I haven't wanted to deal with it. I'll do the plan."

I thanked him, I talked to his wife, and the plan was put in place.

Long story short, he and his family are fine now. It took a lot of effort and courage for him to deal with his insides and his outsides at the same time, but he did the work.

He would tell you that the thing that turned the corner was when I told him to stop talking. I didn't know it would have that effect;

I was just feeling desperate. But he said that it forced him to stop minimizing how scared and miserable he really was and face how things were. After that, he came to grips with reality and took the right action steps.

Remember, challenge is more initiated by another person and seldom requested. So don't wait for someone you know who is driving their business, marriage, or health off a cliff to ask you to challenge them. Have the talk. If you have a substance abuser in your life, you understand this.

Some people do request it, however, and that is very helpful. A company I worked with for years had challenge as one of their core values, and they do not fail to challenge each other's ideas in a direct but healthy way. It has made them who they are, which is very successful.

Recently, my family and I were at dinner with friends, and I asked if I could present a mock-up of an assessment tool I had been developing to help people know themselves better. It's called the Townsend Personal and Relational Assessment Tool (TPRAT), and it's based on my model of personal and professional growth. They agreed and I put it on the big TV monitor. Then, for about fifteen minutes, people not only said what they liked about it but also said how the graphics needed work, how the fonts weren't right, how the overall look wasn't what it should be.

I felt the urge to say, "C'mon, guys, it's really early stage. Be nice!" But I had asked for it, and I knew that the more truth I received, the better the product would be. So I kept listening and taking internal notes. On the way home, Barbi said, "Good job not being defensive." I didn't tell her my lip was bleeding from biting it.

Sometimes people use the phrase "push back" to challenge an idea. It is a good substitute and feels more relational in some settings.

When you are challenging someone, they may tell you that you are judging them. If they do that, just say, "Sorry, I want to have a judgment-free relationship with you, so I don't want you to feel that way. Can you do me a favor? Can you tell me how to tell you some perception I have that you may not agree with?" Sometimes it's good to put the ball in the other person's court and simply ask them *how* you can challenge them. A small minority might say, "I don't want to hear perceptions that I don't agree with," and they are hopeless at that point. But most people will offer something like, "Tell me something good about myself" or "Tell me you are on my side" or "Let me know you understand what I'm going through." And when they do, be happy to adapt to them and oblige their request. Challenge is just frightening for some people to metabolize, at least until they experience the benefits.

Challenge, done in love, is a game-changing nutrient and will help you. As with all of the Q4 nutrients, keep your focus on changed behavior. The action steps of changed behavior are the desired outcomes. "Let us consider how we may spur one another on toward love and good deeds" (Heb. 10:24).

Sample: "I need to push back on your statement that people need to trust their kids, and they will do the right thing. Love may be free, but trust is earned. I am concerned that this is why your daughter is sneaking out so much."

DEVELOPMENT

Development has to do with being trained for something. It is guiding another to structured growth in some area. It is creating a path to do something which you can't do today. Here are some examples.

- ▸ Joining a parenting class
- ▸ Taking on an executive coach
- ▸ Going through lessons in spiritual direction
- ▸ Joining a leadership peer group for professional growth
- ▸ Getting counseling to understand your insides better
- ▸ Taking lessons in guitar, golf, singing, or rock climbing
- ▸ Learning systematic theology
- ▸ Grooming for a different career

In all of these examples, there are elements common to development.

▶ *Focus.* A targeted area of improvement, limited to that area
▶ *Information.* Books, videos, feedback that provide the data you need
▶ *Guidance.* A person who can coach you and walk through the process with you
▶ *Experiences.* Skills, examples, and trainings to make it personal and real
▶ *Goals.* Some way to know that you are improving in the area
▶ *Customization.* A way to make it fit you and your context

Whatever your interest, just make sure you have these six elements in place.

When we aren't growing, we are declining. There is no status quo. That is why being engaged in self-development in anything meaningful is so helpful, and why it qualifies as a relational nutrient. Just as a nutrient is not a luxury but a necessity, without which we have problems, when we are not doing something that is important and interesting to us, our brains, bodies, and organizations tend to atrophy. This action-based nutrient creates energy and a fresh look on life.

A client of mine, Jillian, who owns a company in the medical field, is highly invested not only in her own development but in that of her staff as well. I have seen her take concepts she is learning about growth, leadership, organizational structure, strategy, culture, boundaries, and personal vulnerability and teach them to her people. When I have met with her teams, not only can they spit out the concepts, but they are using them to grow and improve the company.

One of her employees, Valerie, began years ago as a receptionist. But Jillian saw potential in her that was special. Valerie did her job well. She learned. She asked for more to do. She was inquisitive. She asked questions about the mission of the company, as she deeply believed in it. She read books Jillian suggested.

Around this time, Jillian felt a passion to provide a structured development program for Valerie. It was clear to her that Valerie was a person worth investing in. She provided personal mentoring, courses, conferences, and a plan for growth. Valerie ate it up.

Valerie is now the COO of the company. Jillian doesn't know what the next season will be for her. Valerie could leave for a better-fitting opportunity. She could end up running the company when Jillian decides to groom a successor. But one indication of Jillian's character is that she supports Valerie's development whether she stays or goes. Jillian is just happy she had the opportunity to take Valerie to much higher levels of performance and accomplishment. That is her reward.

You may not need some boot camp experience with lots of rigor, intense goals, and a thousand hours of self-sacrifice. For you, development may be getting involved in online family genealogy, having fun with tying the past to the present, and communicating with others about this. But you need something. We all need training. "Praise be to the LORD my Rock, who trains my hands for war, my fingers for battle" (Ps. 144:1). Keep winning the war against entropy, atrophy, and a declining life.

It's a good idea to do a gut check on this nutrient for yourself. Some people read about development and feel overwhelmed, burdened, or just fatigued. Their lives are so busy, full, and perhaps unmanageable that the idea of signing up for some sort of structured growth is far from what they feel they really need, which is more sleep and a vacation.

If that is the case, it's usually not because you are a lazy person. My experience is that you may need to have better boundaries and carve out time and energy for yourself. Just that little pruning can give you some curiosity and drive to find something you can grow and improve in.

Finally, if you are helping others as a leader, parent, or friend, you may not be the person taking them through the development process. The area may not be one you have enough skill in, or you just may not have the bandwidth. But take ownership of being the conduit of the nutrient. Help them find the right people and organizations that will help them engage. Simply showing interest in them and finding sources that can help them is a nutrient of growth in and of itself.

Sample: "Does our company provide development opportunities? If it doesn't, can you coach me informally for professional growth? If you can't, can you refer me to people outside the company who can coach me?"

SERVICE

Our son Ricky works with a consulting company. The leadership of the company is committed not only to high performance and healthy culture but also to community service, as a natural overflow of success and as an important value. Community outreach is also important to Ricky, so it is a good fit.

He told me that, as many companies are starting to do now, the company asks its employees to take two paid volunteer hours a month to invest in doing the community service of their choice, within some parameters set by the organization. Since the company began this initiative, they have discovered positive shifts in their performance indicators.

While these results might be counterintuitive, they are backed by research. We are finding that the brain gets happy and then more productive when we are engaged in altruism, or providing something of value without a tangible return. And that is what the service nutrient is all about. It is guiding others to engage in giving back to the community and the world.

Service is a true relational nutrient. This is because when we do something for another, just because they need it and are without, our brain releases oxytocin, the "cuddle hormone." Oxytocin is a mood elevator and makes us feel more positive and hopeful. Many times, I have been driving home from some ministry or service organization I'm helping with and find that I'm just feeling good, like the world's a decent place and someone is better off now and in some small way, I was part of God's big plan to make things better. And the next thought I invariably have is, *I'm going to do this again.*

So in a way, God has set up in our minds a positive reinforcement program. Doing good creates feeling good, which increases the probability of doing good again.

Service should be done from eagerness, not obligation. Paul writes, "They only asked us to remember the poor—the very thing I also was eager to do" (Gal. 2:10 NASB). So, as with the development nutrient, if you aren't involved and it seems overwhelming, carve out a couple of hours each month. It is almost miraculous how it feels when someone says to you, "I don't know what we would have done without you. Thank you." The oxytocin surge makes the difference. This is truly the nutrient that keeps on giving, and it gives to the giver as well as the receiver.

There are an almost infinite number of ways to help out.

- Mentoring young leaders
- Volunteering at domestic violence shelters
- Giving and traveling to developing countries to help their sustainability
- Teaching kids at church services
- Helping the elderly
- Helping organizations that fight sex trafficking
- Sitting on the boards of organizations that provide for the needy

If you are in a crisis and are struggling to survive, it's probably not the right time to engage heavily in service. Wait until your life is more stable and healthy. But I know so many busy people who have kids, grandkids, demanding jobs, and health issues yet still make service a priority. They just make it part of their life. Sure, they get tired. But so what? They have so many stories to tell me at dinner that are heartwarming and inspiring. In many ways, giving is how life ends up being good.

Sample: "Let me brainstorm with you on getting involved in some sort of community service organization. Our community needs your talents, and I think you will be glad when you see the results."

◆　◆　◆

There you have them. The twenty-two relational nutrients, divided into four quadrants: Be Present, Convey the Good, Provide Reality, and Call to Action. Some combination of these, from the right people, at the right times, in the right amounts, will produce good fruit in your life.

Before we discuss finding the right relationships to provide *you* with these nutrients, take a moment to consider their many uses.

CONSIDER THE PURPOSE

Just like biological nutrients, the relational nutrients have more than one usage and value.

Maintenance. We just need each other in our lives, providing and being provided for, to stay energetic, connected, and productive. You don't want to get mental anemia or bone loss! So stay in touch with the right people and be engaged in the transfer, every week.

You may think, *I'm okay, and I don't have any needs today.* And you may be right. Then give something to the other person.

Let's say you notice something positive in a person that you would like to affirm. They have not asked for affirmation, but you observed something good and tell them. "The way you handled that tough situation with the client was just excellent. Great job."

What happens, metabolically, to that nutrient? It doesn't just disappear inside the person's brain. God is much more efficient than that. It travels from the eyes and ears, landing in the memory banks, where it is stored as a positive and lasting experience. Then, a week later, when the person needs a boost of affirmation because of some new stressor, it can be accessed. The person can think, *I need to know some-one appreciates all I do, because it's been a bad week. But I remember that last week, Walt noticed my work on the tough customer.* The person returns to what that felt like last week and can press on. You never waste a great nutrient. Perhaps the exceptions are in Q3 and Q4, when you might give too much advice or too many challenges. We all need to be careful about that. But I don't think it's possible with Q1 and Q2.

Growth. We all need to grow, in all sorts of areas. We were designed to be more loving, more joyful, better listeners, more honest, and better spouses, friends, parents, leaders, and businesspeople. The nutrients will keep you on your self-improvement path.

Stress relief. In difficult times of pressure, loss, or failure, the nutrients help us persevere and make it through. In these seasons of life, it's critical to receive even higher doses than usual—meaning more time with the right people—to keep you feeling as normal as possible.

Healing. When you have been wounded inside, suffering from isolation, depression, a broken heart, anxiety, or an addiction, you need to be in a healing process. This is certainly a time in which the nutrients must come into play.

The bottom line is, don't wait to get this straight until you are having significant trouble: lack of energy, inability to concentrate, discouragement, money problems, family issues, or business concerns. Don't wait for the physician to say, "If you had come to me sooner, we could have prevented the surgery." Begin taking steps, especially Q1 steps, to get involved in this part of the life that Jesus intended for us. "I came that they may have life, and have it abundantly" (John 10:10 NASB). Abundance can be found in experiencing the right relationships and all that they offer.

This book provides a table summarizing the relational nutrients (p. 81). People have found this list of nutrients useful to refer to when they are headed to a meeting or a conversation. It can be about what you need for yourself, or it can be a guide to what the other person might need.

Also, I suggest Henry Cloud's book *The Power of the Other*. It is a great resource on how important relationships are. In Henry's model of four positions of relatedness, corner 4, which he calls "Good Connection," relates to these quadrants as examples of good relationships.

In the next section, as you engage in the seven Cs of relationships, you will learn how to determine what sorts of people you might need more time with, and what sorts you might need to cut back on.

PART 3

WHO SHOULD DELIVER YOUR NUTRIENTS?

The Seven Cs

You need the highest-grade relational fuel possible to achieve a great life. So it makes sense that you also need to identify the right people to provide you the fuel.

And that is your responsibility. Not every person in the world is the right person to provide you with great nutrients. People may be our primary source of growth, but unfortunately there are some better-qualified people and some less-qualified people. Some have it to give and some don't. Some people, through no fault of their own, simply don't have a lot to provide you. It's not fair to expect someone who is in a personal crisis to spend a lot of energy helping you be more connected and encouraged.

Some of the most successful and healthy people I meet are so clear about this. One told me, "I can always tell if a person is right for me by having lunch with them. With some, I walk away feeling like I can go kick butt in the world. And with others, I need to take a nap to recover from them."

Finding and engaging with the right people is not an accident. It's a mistake to just hope that the people you are around today all have the nutrients you need, and vice versa. Like anything else in life, this is a matter of intentionality, meaning you need to think about this and take some action steps. "Walk with the wise and become wise, for a companion of fools suffers harm" (Prov. 13:20). We will all walk with someone. It may as well be the right someones.

This section has to do with a model of the seven categories, or Cs, that cover the great majority of your relational world. The Cs structure will help you see where you are spending your time in what kinds of relationships. With some people, you will decide, *I need more of this type*. With some, it will be, *Maybe I need fewer of these*. And with others, *What was I thinking?*

Of course, you will see yourself in the seven Cs as well. They will give you a yardstick to help you determine what kind of person you are with others, what nutrients you provide, and how you can have a more positive impact in their lives.

CHAPTER 11

COACHES

Get the Expertise

Often when I speak to leaders, I will start my talk by asking this question: "How many of you have had some kind of coach? It could have been when you were in third grade baseball. Or dance class. Or maybe it was a tutor for algebra. Or a trainer for working out." Most of the time, about 90 percent of the attendees will raise their hands.

Then I will say, "Okay, I want you to think about your all-time favorite coach, whether you were a kid or an adult. The one you respected and received so much benefit from. The one whose time with you helped form the person you are today, and whose impact still helps you. Think about one memory you have of what that person did with you that made all the difference. Just shout it out."

I have kept notes on what I have heard over the years, and there is a great and inspiring variety to the responses. Here are some examples.

- ▶ "He saw something in me that I didn't know I had."
- ▶ "She pushed me to accomplish more than I ever thought was possible."
- ▶ "He cared about me, and it made me a better person."
- ▶ "She knew her area of expertise inside out and loved the subject."
- ▶ "He stuck with me when I won and when I lost."
- ▶ "She explained things to me in a way that made sense to me."

You can easily see the common denominator in all of these statements. It is that the outcome of the relationship is the ability to accomplish at a higher level than before. If these individuals had not had their coaches investing in them, they might have succeeded, but it is highly unlikely that they would have succeeded at the levels they achieved.

And that leads to my definition of a coach: one who takes others down a path of growth and competency in a specific area. Using conversations, empathy, information, challenge, and life experiences, a coach provides the context that brings out not only the best in a person but also what is not yet formed in that person. It is a personal and modeling relationship. Paul wrote, "The things you have learned and received and heard and seen in me, practice these things, and the God of peace will be with you" (Phil. 4:9 NASB).

The second thing you'll notice in these statements is that the coaching was tailored to the person, not the reverse. Some people were motivated by the coach's belief in them, some by challenge, some by competence. Coaching is a very personal experience, and while there are universals to it, the best coaches always adapt to what their coachee needs in order to be the best they can be.

There are many shadings of the coaching relationship. Here are just a few examples.

- ▶ Personal or life coaches, who focus on overall personal, family, and career health
- ▶ Mentors, who use their experiences to help others
- ▶ Executive coaches, who concentrate on helping leaders increase performance
- ▶ Spiritual directors, who guide individuals into a deeper relationship with God
- ▶ Therapists, who help people deal with their emotional, behavioral, and cognitive struggles
- ▶ Workout trainers, who increase strength, tone, flexibility, and functionality

▶ Nutritionists, who have information on the food and supplement balances a person needs

▶ Sports coaches, who take athletes to new levels of achievement

▶ Music coaches, who help the musically gifted to excel

I have had great coaches in all areas of my life for many years, and I plan to continue this indefinitely. I can't even measure their impact in my life, except to say I am convinced that because of these people, I am *much* farther down the road in being who God created me to be, and I am thankful for them. "Let the wise listen and add to their learning, and let the discerning get guidance" (Prov. 1:5).

I began my graduate work in seminary, and by the time I was a year from graduating, I planned to be a missionary. I had always been interested in missions and felt I had the right skills for the job. However, a faculty member of the seminary, Dr. Frank Wichern, who was a psychologist and knew my bachelor's was in psychology, invited me to attend a process group of seminary students. I agreed, not really knowing what the term process group means. Maybe some sort of mutual encouragement thing or an accountability group?

My world was rocked by my experience in that group. Frank was, and is, a master of the science of group processing. He helped create a safe place for us, allowed us to be vulnerable, and helped us experience together God's grace and truth. I saw breakthroughs, transformations, marriages healed, and careers launched.

After several months, I realized I had a deep passion and interest—deeper than I could have imagined—in the work of helping people grow on a personal level. I felt more called to this path than to missions. Times of reflection and prayer, and conversations with friends, helped to confirm this.

So I told Frank, "I want to do this for a living."

He said, "Sounds like a good idea. You'd probably do well in this area."

"Great," I said. "How do I start? I suppose after I graduate, I get some office space and start marketing my services?"

"Actually, no. To do this right, you'll need to go to another five years of grad school and earn a doctorate in psychology."

I thought about his answer, then asked, "What's plan B?" I really didn't want to get more schooling. I wanted to start my career.

"I don't know, but this is my recommendation for you."

Oh well.

So after more thought and conversations, I agreed with Frank's suggestion, drove to California—which I had never been to in my life—and spent the next few years earning my PhD. It turned out to be one of the best decisions I have ever made, as the combination of learning theology and psychology gave me a biblical and conceptual foundation for all the books I have written and all the contributions I have made. I don't recommend that everyone who is in my space get a doctorate, as it is often not necessary. But for what I needed to accomplish in my personal mission, it was the right thing.

This is what I mean by the impact of a coach. Frank knew me well enough to push me in this direction, even though it was a challenge, and I will always be grateful for his impact.

COACHING IS WORTH IT

It takes time, energy, and often money to have a coach. Is it worth this kind of investment? If it's the right person and you are in the right place, I think so. Let's look at the reasons.

Coaching is now part of our culture and our everyday conversation. Google "coach" and you will get an enormous number of hits. This is no promise that it works, but the millions of people who report benefits from coaching does say something.

You will not see a professional athlete competing on the world stage who doesn't have a coach. It is now simply a necessary part of that person's development. The same is true with the arts, the sciences, and any other area of professionalism.

In the business and leadership world, coaching has grown very quickly as an industry over the past few years. It is now routinely a part of the organizational experience, the family growth world, and the personal growth arena.

In a study of coaching in the professional world, conducted by PricewaterhouseCoopers and the Association Resource Centre, most of the companies surveyed reported that their median returns were seven times the cost of the coaching.[4] Other, ongoing studies in the business world support the idea that coaching brings value.

A few decades ago, if a CEO was given a coach, that was a sign that she was struggling and needed remediation. It was not seen positively. Nowadays, however, as organizations and leaders have experienced the benefits, coaching is often included in the comp package as one of the perks of being a leader.

The world of the personal, or life, coach has also grown a great deal. People find help and movement from someone who knows what they are doing and wants to motivate them to take some step or path that will get them from point A to point B. That was Frank's help for my situation.

In my own efforts as a coach, I have worked with thousands of individuals and have trained a number of professional coaches, and it has produced the right kind of fruit. You often don't know the endgame in a coaching relationship, the move that really makes the difference.

One client, a small business owner in the transportation industry, came to my program for help in increasing the performance and profit of his business. We worked on task-based issues such as vision alignment, organizational structure, and a coherent strategic plan. All of these helped. But during that time, we discovered also that his leadership skills were limited because of his tendency to micromanage others, taking over when he needed to remove his hand from the wheel. The employees with the potential to take the company to scale would get frustrated and leave, which created a vicious cycle, because then he would take over even more.

So we got to work on what was going on inside him that drove that behavior. We uncovered a difficult childhood with his harsh father. This influenced him not to trust anyone but himself. Trust, in his internal world, led to disaster. Obviously, this then led to serious problems in delegation. As I have a holistic approach, which deals with both the personal and the task-based areas of life, we were able to make significant progress in this arena as well. He improved greatly in letting others handle what they could handle, and the company did very well.

Think back to when you had a challenge in some arena and didn't have someone with expertise, someone who had been there, to help. It's no fun to feel that you have to soldier through life alone, finding your way through areas that have already been successfully navigated by others.

And think about the fueling and relational nutrients that can be delivered by a coach. The small business owner I coached experienced all four quadrants.

- ▶ *Quadrant 1: Be Present.* We had many conversations in which his frustration with his performance, as well as his fear of trusting, were validated.
- ▶ *Quadrant 2: Convey the Good.* He was very hard on himself and often despaired that he would ever lead his company the way he should. He received affirmation that he was working on the right issues that would lead to the right solution.
- ▶ *Quadrant 3: Provide Reality.* He gained more understanding of how his company needed a leader who could stick with his CEO role and let go of other roles so that his employees could develop.
- ▶ *Quadrant 4: Call to Action.* He was given a road map for how to craft both the right kind of organizational structure and the strategy that emerged from that.

Over and over, coaches deliver the nutrients we need to grow.

THE THREE ATTRIBUTES OF A COACH

The science of coaching comes down to three capacities that all great coaches have.

Subject matter expertise. This is pretty obvious. A coach needs to know the subject you are interested in improving in. She needs to know more, a lot more, than you do, meaning she is a subject matter expert (SME). Think of Malcom Gladwell's ten-thousand-hours concept from his book *Outliers*: people who do very well at something have spent an enormous amount of time perfecting their skill, from Bill Gates to the Beatles to Pelé. So an executive coach must have a deep knowledge of leadership and organizations. A life coach must understand what makes people overcome obstacles and succeed.

Most of us don't have ten thousand hours to study and train on a subject. It just makes sense to be mentored by another person who can share his expertise. The outsourcing is worth it.

I was meeting with the founder of a group of social services organizations. With us was a mutual friend who is very strong in the family ministry world and had introduced the two of us. The founder and I talked about his social services enterprise. I have a lot of interest in how organizations are structured and what their strategies consist of. So I went to the whiteboard wall in my office that I use for creating concepts and began making diagrams with him about how his companies work. We went to some depth into the intricacies of how he does what he does.

Our mutual friend told me later how much he enjoyed watching us, but he confessed he knew very little about what we were discussing. I said, "If I were in your office, watching you strategize about how to help families grow and thrive worldwide, I'd have the same experience." It's all about the subject matter expertise.

Coaching competence. It's not enough to know an area well. Lots of people are experts, but they are poor coaches. Not every pro golfer would be a great coach, nor every senior pastor, nor every salesperson. It is a common problem in business when a company wants to promote an SME to management and it doesn't work. He may be the best of the best in his area, but he has few capacities to train others.

Coaching is a set of skills, in and of themselves, distinct and different from an SME capacity. The coaching profession itself is made up of SMEs in coaching. Here are some of the skills that create a great coach, no matter what the arena.

- ▶ *Connecting.* This requires the capacity to forge a relationship of trust with the coachee.
- ▶ *Goal setting.* Knowing how to find what results will give the coachee the outcome they are interested in.
- ▶ *Creating a path.* Helping the coachee know the necessary steps to get there.
- ▶ *Resourcing.* The ability to help the coachee find the necessary time, information, and support.
- ▶ *Questioning.* Great coaches often ask why, to uncover deeper issues that are keeping the coachee from going where they want to go.
- ▶ *Solving underlying obstacles.* The capacity to address what is going on underneath and help provide answers. The story of my client in the transportation industry discovering his trust issues is an example. We didn't know that was an obstacle at the time, but we found out, the more time I spent with him.
- ▶ *Providing accountability.* A basic but critical skill, because all of us are busy and tend to lose focus, or we become afraid to push ahead on difficult tasks.
- ▶ *Measuring.* Helping the coachee see what worked and what didn't work, to keep fine-tuning the process.

Some coaches have undergone formal training to gain these competencies. They enter a program, join an association, or attend conferences. This provides them with a more structured and integrated approach to learning their craft. The Townsend Institute provides both a master's degree and a certificate in executive coaching and consulting. There are many excellent programs available.

Some coaches take an organic route. They form their own program. Usually these individuals are more advanced and mature, so they have more access and experience in what they need to work on, and they have a large network of professionals they can engage with for help.

And some coaches create a hybrid of both formal training and organic training. However it works, if you are looking for a coach, make sure you ask about their training, so you get a sense of where they have been.

Autonomy. This third attribute may be my favorite one. A great coach needs to be someone friendly, someone you like, but on their part, they have no need for you to be their best friend. To be autonomous means to be free; in this case, the coach is free from wanting your support and help. And that frees you up.

You have probably had a number of lunches with someone from whom you wanted support or information and realized that half of your time together was spent on their challenges in life and work. It's a great experience to be able to get on the phone with your coach, say hi and ask how they are, and then say, "What I want to talk about today is . . ." And the rest of the time is all about you! That may sound selfish, but it isn't. It is part of the relationship, just like the time you spend with your doctor or your car repairman. The coaching paradigm creates this sort of expectation.

WHERE'S YOUR COACH?

Most of us aren't high-level athletes or musicians. But all of us need coaching of some sort, either in work or in our personal lives, or both. Here are some ways to locate a coach who can make all the difference.

▶ *Ask around.* If you have a friend or a colleague who is doing well or growing in an area that you want to improve in, just check in with them and ask. The questions "Do you have a coach?" or "Do you know of a coach?" are simply normal things people ask these days. Word of mouth from someone who is experiencing benefit is generally a good referral.

▶ *Check with your church or your company.* Organizations have access and information regarding people who coach and mentor that is above and beyond an individual's reach. Healthy churches, especially, often have vetted lists of people who have some expertise and would like to give back to others wanting to grow, and they provide a pro bono service that can be very helpful.

▶ *Inquire with coaching organizations.* An online search in your area of interest will almost assuredly come up with groups that provide coaches. Coaching is now a multibillion-dollar industry, so they are out there.

The subtitle of this chapter is "Get the Expertise." This is because it just makes sense, as a first step in utilizing the right sources of the right nutrients, to engage with someone who has been where you want to go. You will find direction, avoid missteps, and gain focus for your life and work. Being coached is a key part of the growth you seek and need.

CHAPTER 12

COMRADES

Build Your Life Team

Randall, a successful business owner in his late thirties, retained me to help keep his personal and professional lives healthy, balanced, and productive. My protocol with this sort of assignment is to spend a day with the client, doing what is called a needs analysis. A needs analysis is sort of a life report card, to determine areas of strength and areas that need improvement.

At the end of the day, we reviewed the analysis. "You are doing a lot of things right," I said. "You run your company well. You have a wonderful marriage and family. Your faith life is vibrant. You eat right and work out. You are a generous philanthropist, and you have lots of friends."

He said, "Thanks" and was happy about that. However, being a perceptive person, Randall added, "Okay, but what's the but?"

I said, "The but is that you have what I call a relational deficit. You don't have enough of the right kinds of relationships with the right kinds of people to keep your life optimized." I had explained the concept of relational nutrients to Randall, so he was aware of what they were.

He was curious about this. "What does 'relational deficit' mean? I have a great set of friends."

"You do," I agreed. "But you aren't engaging with them on some sort of structured level for self-improvement and growth."

"Well, that's why I hired you as a coach. Plus, I have God and my family and my small group from church."

"Yes, you do. You have a lot of good growth things going. But I don't think you are getting the best outcomes from all of this, to be all you want to be. A small group is great, and I have been in one myself for many years. It's an important part of my life. But most small groups focus on a book or Bible study as the main thing; conversations about personal and relational growth are secondary. And lots of the time, the membership is assigned, rather than the individual picking his own people. These aren't good or bad aspects, just apples and oranges.

"First, I'd like to propose that you set up what I call a Life Team. Briefly, the term refers to an intentionally selected set of people who become your primary source for relational nutrients. You may study the Bible or a book with these people. But the main focus is growth—specifically, transferring the relational nutrients to one another, resulting in doing better in your personal, relational, spiritual, and emotional life.

"Second, you are a leader. One thing I have found about leaders is that they end up leading the groups they join. It isn't intentional. It's just that they have a certain skill set, and groups need someone to lead, and there is this vacuum that gets filled by the leader, which everyone generally goes along with. So how many small groups have you been in that you end up leading in some way?"

"All of them," Randall said.

"Right. And I'm sure you do a great job and are happy to help. But lots of leaders I work with tell me that they'd like a space to fill up their own gas tanks. So a Life Team structure is set up so that everyone gets the benefit. It is a mutual transfer of nutrients, not a delivery of nutrients from leader to group."

Randall thought about it and liked the idea. It all came together quickly, because he already had five close friends that he wanted to recruit to a Life Team. I wrote up a description of the process, very close to what is in this chapter, and he got 100 percent buy-in.

They have been meeting regularly for several years now, and they all would tell you that the structure has been transformational for them.

Ask yourself, "Do I have a reliable and quality source to provide me with the twenty-two relational nutrients on an ongoing basis?" Most people I talk to will say they do not. They have friends, people to have spiritual growth experiences with, confidants, and the like. But they don't have this sort of arrangement.

LIFE TEAMS

A Life Team is composed of those individuals who know all about you and can handle it all, just as you know and can handle everything about them. They aren't coaches, as coaches are people you retain for your growth, not theirs. That is why the word comrades fits. They are in it for the mutual growth process.

A Life Team is basically the highest and best set of friendships, at least in the way that Jesus described it. "I no longer call you servants, because a servant does not know his master's business. Instead, I have called you friends, for everything that I learned from my Father I have made known to you" (John 15:15). These are friends who know your business, making you fully known and fully loved, with no secrets or hiding.

A Life Team is also a structure which embodies family. We are all born into, or raised in, a family or a family setting. God created family to develop and grow little people so they become larger people called adults. We usually call this family the family of origin (FOO).

We are all to give respect to and love our families of origin. Many of them have lots of good to them, which we are to be grateful for, and some amount of dysfunction. Unfortunately, some have more dysfunction than good. Either way, they deserve our kindness, even when we are learning to set limits, forgive, and heal from the negatives.

However, the Bible teaches that God has created a second and superior family. It consists of those people who may not be biologically related to you or may not have raised you but during your adult years have loved, accepted, nurtured, and developed you. This second family often serves to complete the work that was not done by a person's family of origin.

- ▶ Providing security, when there was little
- ▶ Making attachment and vulnerability safe, when it was in short supply
- ▶ Giving them structure and a sense of self-discipline, so that they don't lose themselves in impulses and distraction
- ▶ Helping them find their voice and boundaries, when they had learned to comply and be passive
- ▶ Showing them that their dark side and failures are understood and accepted, rather than ignoring, withdrawing from, or judging these aspects
- ▶ Helping them be kind to themselves about their mistakes instead of harshly judging themselves
- ▶ Showing them how to accept their negatives rather than hiding in entitlement and narcissism
- ▶ Providing them with the ability to relate to others as adults
- ▶ Giving them confidence to develop and express their God-given talents, rather than telling them to be someone they are not
- ▶ Helping them to find their mission and vision for life, rather than leaving them alone to work it out

Jesus validated the existence and importance of this second family. When someone told him that his mother and brothers were waiting to speak to him, he made a startling declaration. "'Who is my mother, and who are my brothers?' Pointing to his disciples, he said, 'Here are my mother and my brothers. For whoever does the will of my Father in heaven is my brother and sister and mother'" (Matt. 12:48–50).

In essence, Jesus was affirming the second family as the more transcendent set of people. Those who do the will of God are that family.

The church is certainly that family, as it was designed to do God's will and fulfill his mission. It is the family of God (FOG), the family that will carry us into growth and health for the rest of our life on earth. And on a smaller scale, the Life Team is a microcosm of this family.

The FOO has a time limit of sorts. We were not designed to stay emotionally or financially dependent on the FOO forever. Instead we are to take the gifts and character that it gave us and launch into the world, doing good and expanding God's kingdom in work, career, love, and ministry. "That is why a man leaves his father and mother and is united to his wife, and they become one flesh" (Gen. 2:24). Called the leaving and cleaving principle, this can apply not only to marriage but also to finding one's social support and growth system. We move from dependence on the FOO to interdependence with the FOG.

I suggest that a Life Team consist of somewhere between three and ten individuals. This is the ideal range, I have noticed over the years. It seems to work best. Too few people, and you don't have the variety of nutrient sources you need. Too many, and you don't have time to go into depth with them.

Certainly, there are FOO members who might be part of your Life Team. If they possess the following eight qualities, there is no reason for them not to be. These individuals have a history of experiences with you that can help both of you. However, if the majority of the members of your Life Team are FOO, it is a yellow flag that the leaving and cleaving has not been completed. Plus, you are limited in the range of relational nutrients you can receive from others.

It is ideal for one's spouse to be on one's Life Team as well. That sort of closeness and vulnerability, combined with shared values, was always God's design, so that couples could be a great source of growth for each other. However, in significantly broken marriages, those qualities may be missing. If that is the situation, one needs to do whatever one can to help heal matters, so that the spouse can one day be part of one's growth.

When seeking Life Team partners, here are the qualities to look for, in no particular order.

Shared essential values. Values are fundamental beliefs about life that serve as a compass for our path and decisions. I worked out a set of personal core values which I have used for many years. (I wrote about this in my book *Leading from Your Gut.*) If you have not thought through your own essential values, I suggest you do that. It will clarify things for you. Feel free to use all of mine, cherry-pick from my list, or have your own completely different set.

A Life Team works better if the fundamentals are essentially agreed on. There should always be room for differences and for changing one's perspective; that is just healthy growth. But if there are great differences in the essentials, you can end up with time-wasting discussion or with a person whose core views are so different from yours that you can't easily receive relational nutrients. There are many people in the world who, for their own reasons, don't think relationship, truth, or growth are all that important. And while they are individuals I would hopefully care about, engage with, and have a good relationship with, knowing I certainly have many flaws myself, they would probably not be people I would invite to be on my Life Team. This is not judgment at all. This is addressing the reality that there are only so many seats on the bus.

Leave room for different preferences and styles. Don't leave room for differing principles. Disagreeing on minor spiritual ideas, politics, culture, and personality styles is fine. There should be no compromise about relationships, truth, and growth.

Engagement in growth on some structured level. A Life Team member needs to be committed to self-improvement, and doing something about it. Their calendar should reflect some commitment to continuously becoming a better person. They may have a coach, mentor, spiritual director, counselor, or small group. But they are putting energy into some source of information and experience that leads to change. There are lots of really good people who are loving and caring, but they aren't intentional about growth. That is no criticism of them at all. They have their own paths and reasons. But a desire to be a better person next year than you are this year, in some significant area, is important for a well-functioning Life Team.

They don't have to be involved in a structure of growth. Your invitation may be the first thing they have considered. But they need to be open to this and able to commit to it. (I designed the Townsend Leadership Program with this approach in mind. It's a turnkey structure for holistic growth that resolves common challenges both personally and professionally. More information about the program can be found in the back of the book.)

A stance of "for." Life Team members need to be oriented to seek each other's best, no matter what. There must be no condemnation or judgment of one another. When you are for someone, your highest value for them is that you provide good for them, in whatever form they need. You can certainly disagree and have differences. But ultimately, Life Team members need to know and experience that they are on each other's side and have their backs.

One of the members of my Life Team had a serious problem in business and made some poor choices with money. It was destructive to his marriage. But he felt safe enough with us that he didn't hide or minimize matters, and he told us how bad things were. We confronted the issues head-on, and there were very direct conversations. But he never felt an ounce of condemnation. Finally, he resolved the matter and turned the business around. And now, when that time comes up in conversation, he is comfortable talking about it, with no shame, guilt, or resentment. That is what living in "for" will do for you.

Vulnerability. To be vulnerable is to be open about negatives in one's life. There are five arenas of vulnerability.

- ▶ *Mistakes.* Those decisions which were the wrong ones
- ▶ *Struggles.* Ongoing situations that are difficult
- ▶ *Weaknesses.* Personal flaws that take time to resolve
- ▶ *Needs.* What we require from others to survive and grow, the relational nutrients
- ▶ *Emotions.* Feelings, which are riskier to talk about than thoughts

The irony of life is that our vulnerabilities are the most important parts of ourselves to express, and the most difficult parts to express. Vulnerability is the avenue to intimacy, sharing nutrients, getting our needs met, growth, and so much more. It is the way we were designed to live: naked and unashamed (Gen. 2:25).

However, sin caused our vulnerability to produce great shame, guilt, anxiety, and fear of rejection. So what we need most is what we also fear most. "Then the eyes of both of them were opened, and they realized they were naked; so they sewed fig leaves together and made coverings for themselves" (Gen. 3:7).

A person who wants to be vulnerable but has a hard time with it is probably okay to be a Life Team member. The value they place on vulnerability indicates that they want to work at it. But a person who sees vulnerability as something to be avoided is probably not ready for this arrangement.

I was working with a group of leaders who wanted to grow deeper on a personal level. They became more open with each other than they were with just about anyone else in their lives. One of them, a very successful CEO whom the others looked up to, said after a few sessions, "I think I need to tell you that I have debilitating anxiety that I will fail in my company and my career, and I haven't told anyone about it." The group was surprised that someone who had performed at very high levels would feel that. But they rallied around him, accepted him and his paralyzing anxiety, and helped him work through it. He is a different person now.

I asked him later, "What do you think would have happened if you hadn't opened up that day?"

He said, "I would have left in a few sessions. I could feel the safety around me, and at the same time, the shame inside me. The tension between the two was tearing me up. I just would not have been able to tolerate it for very long."

I have seen the simple capacity of vulnerability do miracles in people's growth, time after time after time. You don't need to have all the answers. If the room is a safe place, just default to vulnerability.

Truthfulness. Truthfulness is just a no-compromise principle. Truth is how we find answers, discover solutions, and get the feedback we need. Life Team members need a deep commitment to the truth, even if it is disruptive.

This applies to both the personal and the professional dimensions. On a personal level, we know each other only to the extent that we are honest with each other. When deception or dishonesty comes into the picture, the knowing in a relationship has ended. I worked with business partners dealing with a situation in which one made a decision involving allocations of significant funds that, unfortunately, he did not let the other partner know about. When we had the come-to-Jesus meeting, the aggrieved partner said to the other one, "The worst part of this is that I don't know you. I thought I did, but I do not." Having to face this consequence of what he had done bothered the deceptive partner a great deal, and it was a rift that never healed. Health and growth happen when you commit to reality and to being as honest as possible.

Mutuality. You are all in the process together. Everyone brings his or her wins and losses to the meeting and transfers the relational nutrients back and forth where they are needed. One member might have a facilitative role, making sure that the agenda is followed and keeping time. Or those chores may rotate. Sometimes there is no real agenda, just an open group, depending on preferences. There are some structures in which there is a dedicated facilitator whose purpose is to teach or keep the conversation going. But that person usually should not be a part of the group in terms of sharing and vulnerability. It is hard to lead others and get your own needs met at the same meeting. It can be confusing as to whose needs are being met.

When I am working with leaders, I will often start with, "Okay, take off your leadership hats now," as the tendency to run things and provide answers and guidance is usually strong. With the leadership hats off, the "one anothers" in the Bible are expressed in a vulnerable and productive way.

This also means that over time, each person's give and take is proportional. Everyone's needs and challenges use about the same amount of bandwidth in meetings and conversations. We all have our seasons of trouble, and in those times we require more of the spotlight. But if one person's needs or crises constantly hijack the group's time, you will need to help that person find supplemental support (a therapist, a coach, a second support group) so that they have more resources and can function more mutually as a Life Team member. In some rare circumstances, it might mean that a person's situation is simply too severe for them to be able to reciprocate. In those cases, they may need to be more of a care relationship for you (which I'll discuss a few chapters from now) than a comrade connection.

Chemistry. It's important that you like your Life Team members. It may not be essential, but it certainly helps. If you don't have chemistry with another person, it can be drudgery and obligation. If I thought that every meal I ate would have to be some vegetable that I can't stand, I would dread eating in general. You don't want to drive to your lunch with a Life Team member, thinking, *I'm sure she is good for my growth, but being with her is a workout.* Much better to think, *I've been waiting all week to download life with her!*

Availability. This is the simple logistical part. You and the members of your Life Team must be available to have meaningful conversations with each other. That is the only way to experience the right amounts of nutrients. You can't take your daily supplements all at one time on January 1 and expect them to work for the year. The bloodstream needs to metabolize the ingredients at a certain rate, and it's the same for relational nutrients.

My rule of thumb is that monthly is probably the least frequent structure for meetings, either as individuals or as a group. Otherwise, a great deal of time is spent playing catch-up on the events of life, rather than doing the work of vulnerable growth. This is not hard and fast. But if you have a very close friend with whom you talk only a couple of times a year, and a pretty close friend you can talk with every couple of weeks, the latter frequency of connection is more effective for you. Keep the very close friend; never leave that relationship! But consider that a different relationship than a Life Team connection.

You may already be in some sort of structured growth context: a small group, life group, Bible study, or the like. There is no reason that this group can't use the elements of a Life Team. But consider whether the members want to make the transfer of relational nutrients a priority. It's also a good conversation to have with them. You may not have to start from scratch. I have seen an ongoing group prioritize the exchange of relational nutrients, and I have seen groups whose members feel it's not something they have the bandwidth to do.

Most of us also have close friends who matter a great deal to us. We spend time with them and confide in them. A close friend can have most of the qualities of a Life Team member, but for some reason it's not the right fit for you or for them. This is usually not any sort of a value judgment; it's more of a compatibility issue.

In my experience, there are three aspects which differentiate a close friend from a Life Team member.

1. *A commitment to personal growth.* Some people don't feel a need for engaging in activities and conversations for self-improvement. They are just awesome, warm, loving people with whom you enjoy being close.
2. *Vulnerability.* Some close friends can really be there for you, but it is difficult for them to open up about their own insecurities and weaknesses. They are supportive and safe, but it tends to go in one direction—toward you.
3. *Availability.* The logistical reality is that some people who would be great Life Team members don't have time to connect on a regular basis. Maybe they are going through a very busy season of life with family or work activities or challenges.

WHAT ABOUT OPPOSITE SEXES?

I think it's generally a good idea to include opposite-sex relationships (OSRs) in one's Life Team. There are certainly guardrails to put in place in some situations, but for the richest and most effective experience of growth, you can't beat the variety of perspectives, thinking patterns, and life histories of healthy, safe, and growing men and women helping each other improve. If we cut off access to half of the human race, we can be in danger of limiting the good growth nutrients—such as attunement, encouragement, insight, and advice—that healthy OSRs can provide for us.

Countless times, I have heard women give feedback like the following: "You are stonewalling your wife when you shut down from her when you are upset. It hurts her. Take initiative and open up to her." Or a man will tell a woman, "You really wound your husband when you constantly criticize him. I suggest you back off and become more supportive." The credibility of the opposite-sex viewpoint is hard to deny.

One member of a leadership group I led told me, "My wife loves it that my group has women. They basically tell me that she's right, every time we meet!"

There are certainly situations in which OSRs are not a good idea— for example, when a person has been unfaithful and is unrepentant or in denial. These situations need to be taken a case at a time. For more information on this, you can read a position paper that Focus on the Family commissioned me to write on the issue; it is available on their website.[5]

SIMILARITIES AND DIFFERENCES

Should your Life Team be homogenous—with members of similar ages, levels of personal maturity, accomplishments, or industries? Or should it be highly heterogenous, with wide variances among members? Should a twenty-three-year-old who is starting his website have a Fortune 500 CEO as a Life Team partner?

This is a preference question. It comes down to one variable that you need to keep in mind when you consider who you want to be connected to: what do they offer that you need the most, and what do you offer that they need the most? If you need a great deal of insight and feedback from others who are "walking your walk" in your life experience, your Life Team may be more homogenous. But if you find that stretching your perspectives to keep from being stuck in your own point of view is a value, then more variance is the direction you want to consider.

THE AGENDA

There is a great deal of flexibility in choosing the mode of how you connect, ranging from individual conversations to group meetings. Remember that a Life Team may be a group, or it may be a group plus some people who are not in the group, or it may be some individuals with no group. As much as possible, however, go for a group. The power of a group can't be overestimated. But here are examples of the modes.

Group meeting. This can be a weekly, biweekly, or monthly meeting. It can have a great deal of structure or not much. In general, the longer the meeting, the more structure is required. A ninety-minute gathering can just be sharing how life is going, being vulnerable, and supporting one another. It can include prayer and Bible study, but it must allow a significant amount of time for members to talk to one another about their successes, struggles, and failures. So it might be a good idea to have a separate group for a full-on Bible study in which the content of the Bible is the main focus and takes the majority of the time.

Some people prefer a more involved, high-commitment, all-day meeting in which there is high engagement. It can occur monthly, with connections in between. This level of meeting will need to be more structured. Here is an example of the agenda for this sort of group meeting.

1. *Stretch goals.* Annual personal and professional goals that members determine for themselves, that will require support from the team.
2. *Check-in.* A review of each person's highs and lows since the previous meeting, how their stretch goals are progressing, and how any growth homework assignments are coming along, plus a statement of what that person needs from the team this day.
3. *Content.* A lesson on some aspect of growth in spiritual matters, relationships, personal life, or business. It can be a book, a curriculum, a video, or a live speaker. It needs to be highly interactive and relevant to the needs of the team.
4. *Sharing.* A time when the chairs are in a circle, not at a conference table. This is a core element of what a Life Team relationship is about. Members take risks and show who they really are. They open up about needs and challenges and receive nutrients from all four quadrants.
5. *Work issues.* Some all-day leadership meetings of this nature involve members bringing up specific career challenges in areas such as finances, marketing, sales, culture, and teams. They use the group as an ad hoc board of advisers to receive guidance and recommendations.
6. *Aha's and homework.* At the end of the day, each member determines what insight mattered to them about the day (aha), and any action step they need to take before the next meeting (homework). Someone might say, "My aha was that I hold my cards close to the chest and I'm not really open, yet this is a very safe team. I had no idea how careful I have been. My homework is to make some phone calls to the team this month and let them know how I'm really doing, with the good, the bad, and the ugly."

This format is a framework of an agenda my organization uses, which basically functions as a turnkey Life Team structure.

Individual meeting. Just have a regular lunch or coffee with a Life

Team member. Keep in mind, however, that the goal is growth via the transfer of relational nutrients. It's easy to chat about the events of the last couple of weeks, and you do need context with each other. But you want to walk away knowing you have been vulnerable and have received something you needed, and so has the other person. So make that the intentional commitment.

Non-face-to-face engagements. Phone, Skype, and text are all fine sources of growth for your Life Team. So far, the neurological research indicates that face-to-face is still the blue-chip modality, but virtual and digital connections are improving markedly. I recently had a videoconference meeting with a Life Team to see if they could connect, relate on a Q1 and Q2 level, and do more than give each other information and advice. It was highly effective. People were vulnerable, felt safe enough to bring out their emotions and needs, and supported each other.

Email has value, but since it takes a while to send and receive information that way, an email is not as effective as a text. Many leaders I work with have group text strings in which they stay in touch several times a week with short bursts of support, which help their lives, attitudes, energy, and decision making.

PUTTING YOUR LIFE TEAM TOGETHER

I was doing a talk on this, and an attendee raised her hand. "I get this, but what island do I go to, to find these three to ten people? They don't live in my town!"

"Sure they do," I said. "You just haven't known where or how to look."

You may feel like this attendee does. You know you need some people to go deep with and grow. And you may have one trusted confidant. But several may not be your reality. Here is a structure for recruiting the right people that works. Give yourself three months or so to get things together.

Go through your contacts list. I am not kidding here. This is the best place to start. I don't know what the average number of contacts is in the address app in most of our computers. Let's ballpark it at seven hundred. Give yourself a couple of hours and go down the list, with the goal of identifying people who might be a good fit for your Life Team. I have done it myself to beta test it. Check out who you think might have the eight qualities of a member.

You will probably end up with a good number of people—say, twenty. You may also have some surprises, like, *How did that person end up on my contacts list? Time to delete!* Once you have your potentials, run through them and pick three who would be at top of mind.

Reach out. Then choose the first person and simply invite him or her to lunch or coffee. It's a simple thing, something like, "I haven't seen you for a long time, would love to catch up." It's not a great idea to start with, "I've realized I have a relational deficit and I want you and me to engage in a mutually committed structure to grow together." That is just weird.

Be there for the other person's vulnerability. As you are talking, see if they happen to present some struggle in life, such as a work, family, or health issue. You can't control whether this happens, but you can be ready for it. If they do mention something, just get in the well with them and attune to them. Say, "I had no idea about your son being in trouble. I'm really sorry. This must be pretty hard for you." They may never have had someone be empathic with them. You are showing them in the conversation what you value, what you offer, and who you are.

Take a small risk. On your side of it, be vulnerable as well. Just open up something in your life. This is a way to see whether the person is right for you as a member of your Life Team. There are several typical responses to vulnerability, one of which is the one you want.

1. "Can you believe the weather we're having? Anyhow, seen any good movies?" This is called deflection. The person changes the subject from something vulnerable to a safer arena. It is

usually because the individual is uncomfortable with personal vulnerabilities. They may have trouble talking about their own. Or they may not know what to say to help. Obviously, this is not the desired response.

2. "Well, cheer up . . . There's a bright side to everything . . . God will take care of this . . . It's probably just a phase . . . Hang in there . . . You're strong, and you'll be fine." This type of response is an avoidance of the negative. The person just can't be there, and stay there, with struggle. There is a switch in their head that says, "I must put a positive bow on this conversation and end up positively, no matter what." Most of the time, it has to do with an anxiety that a little bit of negative can contaminate things and ruin everything. They are probably a very nice person, but this is not your first-choice response.

3. "Sorry to hear about your son's getting into trouble. Are you praying daily for him and reading the Bible with him? . . . Communication is the key . . . Have some healthy activities you can do with him . . . Get him off digital media and into a gym . . . Change his friends . . . I have a great counselor for him." While this sort of response is well intended, it isn't your desired outcome either. It is advice giving. Advice is a relational nutrient, but it's a Q4 nutrient, and when someone is being vulnerable, it should almost never be the first response. Generally, a default to advice indicates that the person is anxious and needs to fix the other individual. The person is uncomfortable just being present, in a Q1 way, with someone who is hurting.

4. "That reminds me about when our daughter was getting into trouble. It was a hard time for us. I remember the night we had to go pick her up from a party and things were out of control. Then there was another time . . ." While it is nice for a person to identify with your struggle, if that is the first response out of the gate, it is a self-referencing response. The person unconsciously thinks that telling stories about their problems is a way to connect with you, not realizing that it can leave you

with pain inside that needs to be expressed and understood, and you wind up feeling more alone, and obligated to be compassionate to their world of woe.

5. "I didn't know about your son. This has got to be overwhelming for you. How are you doing with all this?" This is the ideal and desired response. It is simply active compassion, especially when the person puts their fork down, looks at you with authentic care, and maybe even leans toward you. This is the true Q1 response. The person is conveying to you that they have capacity and interest in your struggle and are comfortable with it. Realize that someone may stumble in this response and combine it with advice or sound awkward. They may even give you some combination of all of this. That's fine; the person can learn a lot in the processes outlined in this book, as long as you experience something in the Q1 arena from them. What you are looking for is a value in moving toward needs and negatives. It's much easier for a person to be happy about the positives, the wins, and the victories than it is to be hunkered down in the trenches with someone who is overwhelmed and discouraged. But real, true, and growth-providing relationships are forged in those encounters.

Have two more meetings. If the individual gives you some sense of being interested in your struggle and capable of a Q1 response, then have a couple more lunches or coffees with them. You are looking for a trend, not a one-and-done, to determine fitness. In each of the meetings, express a vulnerability. Hopefully, the person will demonstrate their care somehow. By the way, make sure this meeting has to do with their life for half of the time. It's not a coaching or counseling session for you, and you want to let them know that their struggles are important to you as well.

Make the invitation. If all has gone well, then simply let them know what you are doing, with a comment like, "I am becoming more intentional about my personal growth, and focusing on being a better person. In doing so, I want to invite a few people who would be interested in doing that with me and growing together. Is that something you'd be open to?"

The person will most likely say, "I'm interested. How would it work?"

Your answer will depend on the structure you've determined works for you: a small group, one-on-one meetings, or a hybrid. Let's say it's a small group. "I'd like to form a small group, maybe five individuals, who want to get together for more conversations like we are having. We would talk about what's really going on, it would be confidential, no one would be the teacher, and we would all grow together. We might have no agenda except connection. Or we might have some Bible study or go over a book. We might pray together. But whatever we do, the focus would be on being open and vulnerable, supporting each other through good times and tough times, and helping each other with self-improvement."

I have taken many people through this structure. About 90 percent of the time, the response from the individual will be, "Certainly! I don't have anything like this, except with my spouse and another person. I'd be very interested." You have to understand that most people just don't have a structured context that is engineered for the transfer of relational nutrients to foster growth. You are doing them a favor as well as yourself.

BE WHAT YOU REQUIRE

This whole process of assembling your Life Team can sound like the *Ocean's* movies, when either Frank Sinatra or George Clooney puts the team together in Las Vegas to make the heist. Everyone wanted to be with Danny Ocean; in fact, they wanted to *be* Danny Ocean.

But in a Life Team, it's not that way. You have to be humble and vulnerable when you are having your conversations with others. You may not meet the other person's requirements for a Life Team member! So don't come into the setting assuming that they are lucky that you are interviewing them. Be what you require, which is honest and vulnerable and looking for support.

Obviously, there are lots of options to this. It is not manualized at this point. Look at the Life Team concept as the essence of what comrade relationships are all about. You will be pleasantly surprised at the positive responses of people who want to grow, who want to be vulnerable, and who want great relationships.

Note: Another way to experience the power of a group in helping the growth process is to attend a one-week workshop at Growth Skills *(www.growthskills.org)*. This organization trains individuals, leaders, and counselors in an intensive growth process, using materials developed by Henry Cloud, me, and others. Their workshop is a highly effective means of seeing how a team concept can work very well.

In the next chapter, you'll see the advantages of relationships with a different set of people—casuals. We all have casuals, and we all can be good casuals for others.

CHAPTER 13

CASUALS

Make Great Acquaintances

Every day, we encounter people of all sorts in our social lives, in our neighborhoods, through work connections, at sports events, at church, and in organizations we belong to. These are simply people we would call friends or acquaintances. We have lunch with them and see them at parties. And they are also an important part of having the right kind of life. While your Life Team comrades are your deepest commitments, friendships are known by research to be part of longevity, health, and general happiness.

Casuals are low-commitment, enjoyable relationships. They are that neighbor you invite over from time to time for a barbecue and a beer, or that person you have lunch with after church a few times a year. They are those people whose kids are on the same sports teams as yours. Look at it as some combination of "for," mutuality, and chemistry on an informal level.

I have a great casual friend whose world, career, and worldview are very different from mine. He has no real idea of what I do. I know a little of his business. But we like each other. We get together for a meal when we think of it. I doubt seriously if he would ever come close to reading one of my books. We talk about faith matters and discuss religion from time to time. This could not be considered a Life Team relationship or even a close friend. But when I leave a meeting, I always feel pretty energized and happy, and I hope he feels the same way. I haven't asked him.

Casuals can be very important relationships. Casual friends serve several good purposes for you, and you for them.

Living in the present. There are three periods of time: past, present, and future. We can't live in the past; we are only to learn and grow from it. We can't live in the future; we can only plan well for it. God designed us to spend most of our time living in the present, where we can engage in life and make important choices.

Unfortunately, we are an anxious species. With all of the distractions and concerns of life, we tend to get lost in obsessing about yesterday or tomorrow and miss out on today. We forget to be present and mindful of the world that God has given us, right here and right now.

That also applies to nutrients. Relational nutrients can be transferred only in the present, not in the past and not in the future. If you have a vitamin deficiency today, you can't travel to your past in a time machine and take nutrients to prevent the deficiency. Nor can you go to the future and take nutrients and hope they will be effective retroactively. It's all about the now.

That is a great advantage of casuals. They help us to be here and now, in the present. We can watch life go by with a casual and talk about not much at all and come away feeling that we are more ourselves. A good casual friendship helps keep us in balance, away from too much ruminating on the past or worrying about the future.

Differences can be good. When our casuals have different personalities, opinions, styles, values, and tastes, we are better off. Our brain craves experiences that are new and unique and stretch us. They expand our neural network, making new connections. We learn and improve. I have a casual friend who loves weird music, at least weird to me. He plays songs from a huge variety of sources, many from other countries. It keeps me from pigeonholing myself.

A farm team. Your close friends are certainly a source for finding Life Team members. But so are your casuals. Keep your eyes open when you are with them. Look for an opportunity to attune to their lives, and give them an opportunity to respond to your vulnerabilities.

I have seen people find Life Team members among their casuals, like a nugget of gold they discovered that they had no idea was there.

Initiative. Finally, casuals keep us reaching out. We live in a culture nowadays in which so many people don't know their neighbors, the person a few offices down the hall, or the individual next to them in church. Unfortunately, in our society, we can pretty much insulate ourselves from ever having to take initiative to meet new people. With texting, great internet programming, Amazon, and meal delivery, you really don't have to get out of your cocoon. Life is just structured that way. But your brain and your world do better when you develop casuals. And most of them won't introduce themselves to you, for the same reason that you aren't introducing yourself. It won't happen until someone takes the first step.

When Barbi and I moved to our present home years ago, we wanted—as social beings—to be good neighbors. Even though we were the new kids on the block, we felt a responsibility to reach out. Fortunately, we like hosting and parties, so we invited our neighbors to different events at the house. We have found that we are surrounded by wonderful people whom we love to be with. It's worth extending an invitation.

CHAPTER 14

COLLEAGUES

Work Productively and Connected

Work is a central part of life. The great majority of us do something for a living which creates value. Work takes up around half of our waking time, so it is significant, and what we do, whether it be contributing to the provision of a product or a service, matters to our entire mission and direction in life. Moses said to God, "If you are pleased with me, teach me your ways so I may know you and continue to find favor with you. Remember that this nation is your people" (Ex. 33:13). The "ways" that God teaches us include how we work, have jobs, and are productive.

Colleagues, or our work associates, are another kind of relationship which can create a meaningful transfer of relational nutrients. And what we are learning from business and performance research, as well as from neuroscience, indicates how critical relationships are in order for an organization to perform at high levels.

CULTURE

Culture, which I define as how relationships, attitudes, and behavior drive performance, is an obvious arena in which to observe how colleagues can engage at healthy levels. Books like organizational expert Patrick Lencioni's *The Advantage* show, through many case studies, how the people factor is a major part of the success of a company.

You can walk through an office and feel its culture, whether it is warm, cold, fear based, or chaotic. Our son Benny is in commercial real estate finance. He recently changed jobs, taking a better position with a new firm. He asked me to come by and visit the offices. When I took the tour with him, I was met time after time by young, sharp, and authentically friendly associates who took time out to greet me and tell me a bit about what they did. I saw how they engaged with Benny and with each other. I also saw how well they worked and how high-performing they were. I almost asked if I could apply for a job!

If a leader wants to grow the culture of her organization, she must pay attention to the relational nutrients. If the right nutrients are transferred at the right time, not only do people develop individually, but the organization benefits from the health as well. Here are some examples.

- ▶ If a colleague fails or is discouraged in his performance, instead of telling him to be positive and try harder, give him a Q1 nutrient, such as attunement. "I know that losing the account is discouraging for you. You probably feel out of gas, and I get that. I'll help you with this."
- ▶ If a key employee is going above and beyond and just needs to have it noticed, that requires a Q2 response, such as affirmation. "I saw your results on the project, and more important, I have observed all the time and energy you put into it. I'm really proud of your leadership on our team."
- ▶ If an associate is showing signs of not connecting with the team, it may be time for a Q3 transfer, such as insight. "I don't think they see you as personally accessible; from their viewpoint, it's more that you perceive them as a commodity. Do you think that's possible?"
- ▶ If an executive is not focusing on the task and is being distracted from operating on clear priorities, a Q4 response, such

as structure, could help. "I'd like to help you clarify your priorities and work with you on your calendar, so you can spend your time more effectively."

TEAMS

As a key part of the success of an organization of any size, teams also have a high relational component. Look at a team as a "work family" with performance goals. As they learn to share the vision, trust each other, know their roles, and be accountable, they move ahead in the work.

In my experience, probably 80 percent of the reasons a team does not succeed are about relational problems, not task issues. It's the leader's duty to create a context in which people not only are trained, resourced, and given clarity about their roles but also feel they belong and matter.

I consulted with a company which had a horizontal structure. This meant that the staff had a great deal of mutual, rather than command-and-control, interaction with each other. While the company was performing well, the CEO was concerned that the individuals were not using the power of their team as well as they could. They tended to be siloed, reaching out to each other only in perfunctory ways, as in, "How is the project going?" versus "How are the project speed bumps affecting you?"

He decided to have a staff meeting about this, and he told them, "The family I grew up in was a high-performing family. But it wasn't a very connected family. I started this business because, even though my wife and I have formed our own connected family with our kids, I wanted a business which would also be a family. I'm sad that we aren't, and I want to change what I need to change so that we will become not only highly successful but truly vulnerable. And I want to challenge you in that aspect as well."

Silence covered the room for several moments. Then, one by one, people began sharing their desire for having more connection, trust, and vulnerability on their teams.

The company went to work on developing a more relational orientation. In time, the change was transformational, and the performance has increased even more.

PERSONAL AND PROFESSIONAL

Work should not be a source of most of our relational nutrients, especially Q1. This is because work has a performance requirement. We connect at work, but we also must execute there, and at adequate levels. It is hard to consider being deeply vulnerable with someone you report to who will give you a performance review.

There is a difference between what I call personal vulnerability and professional vulnerability. The first is more for your Life Team and close relationships, and the second is fine for work. In a healthy organization, it might be appropriate to share that you are feeling insecure about how your monthly quota went and are questioning yourself. A good supervisor should immediately see that as a real need and help you get back on track. In an unhealthy organization, unfortunately, it might not be safe or appropriate to bring out professional vulnerability, as it could be met with some sort of sanction or criticism. Then your job is to figure out whether the net value of working there is worth it.

For most organizations, it is a judgment call as to whether personal issues such as a divorce or a parenting problem should be brought up. Of course, human resources is always a good source of help. But on a team and reporting-structure level, I have found that when there is high trust, discussing personal issues tends to be a good thing. The only caveat is that the workplace is not where most of the support is. Work is not a primary context for personal growth, counseling, or healing. It is work. The work environment can be a supportive setting, but make sure you are fully utilizing your most important connections elsewhere.

I have many pastor friends and often advise them to find help outside of their work environment, sometimes at another church. It is hard to have a sense of confidentiality and safety if you are a pastor and need to be completely open with someone, when it's all in the same church. I have seen it succeed, but that is more the exception than the rule.

PART OF THE WORK

The nutrients can also play a large part in training staff members, especially those who are outward facing. Relational skills are extremely important when dealing with the public and customers. A good friend of mine who owns a veterinary hospital has established, as part of his professional development protocol for the veterinarians at the organization, training in attunement. They often have to give bad news to a pet owner. Their bedside manner can make all the difference in how the customer experiences the company, and this practice has had a positive impact.

Remember: even when you are focused on your work, relationships matter. You may not be having coffee with someone now, but the coffee you had with them a few hours ago either drained you or energized you for the current task.

CHAPTER 15

CARE

Provide for Others

This is the one category which is designed for more of a one-way transfer of nutrients. The one who is without receives from the one who has. Care is not about you or your needs or your struggles. However, in the way God has designed life and the brain, you do receive something back at a very deep and meaningful level. "If you spend yourselves in behalf of the hungry and satisfy the needs of the oppressed, then your light will rise in the darkness, and your night will become like the noonday" (Isa. 58:10).

A care relationship is one in which you are providing good for those who are without. Look at care as the inverse of the coach category. When you are coached, you are the one in need. When you provide care to someone, they are the one in need. There are several aspects to a care relationship.

They have a legitimate need for some resource that you can provide. There are many needs which can be addressed.

- ▶ Hands-on work in a developing country, helping them with microfinance. Respect, advice, and structure would be some key nutrients here.
- ▶ Providing care for those in domestic violence shelters. Some primary nutrients would be attunement, comfort, and hope.

- ▸ Mentoring a young businessperson in how to succeed in industry. Acceptance, perspective, and feedback would help here.
- ▸ Teaching a kids' Sunday school class. You'd want to include affirmation, perspective, and structure (lots of structure; I did it for years).

When a person cannot provide or create what they need to grow, and there is no manipulation or aversion to effort, it is a legitimate need.

They have no avenue to recompense you financially or otherwise. If they could pay for your help or barter for it, that would make this a simple transaction of services, not a care relationship. That is why most counselors I know have several low-fee slots, as their way of giving back to those who could never afford their help.

The only payment you will receive in a care relationship is an authentic and heartfelt "Thank you." And that has its own rewards. The brain is wired for altruism. When we give from our heart, endorphins are released which provide a pleasant emotional experience. We just feel better.

Your care for them, and their benefit, is the primary focus of the relationship. The focus is on their world, their story, their needs, and their path, not ours. While a care relationship can certainly be a friendship, with a great deal of mutual love and respect, it keeps its focus on the one being cared for.

They take responsibility for the nutrients they are given. A true care person or group does not waste what they are provided. They burn the fuel, using the resources to better their condition, grow, heal, and become more autonomous. They are a very good return on the investment of yourself.

MAINTAINING YOUR PERSPECTIVE

For many, care is part of their wiring. They naturally reach out to others who are without. They have a radar that reads hurt, pain, and distress even when the person in need doesn't mention it. That is a gift.

However, it is also possible to experience what is called compassion fatigue, which is a form of burnout. The condition occurs when a person gives so far beyond themselves that they have a breakdown in some combination of energy, functioning, mood, time, or finances.

If you tend to be vulnerable to compassion fatigue, avoid the thought, *Well, I just love too much.* That is impossible. God himself is love (1 John 4:8), and our highest call is to love. The problem is instead that we go beyond our resources. When that happens, the care goes away and we have to be cared for—not a good use of time and energy.

Here is a simple matrix for determining whether you should care for someone or some organization, and to what extent, and whether you are supporting or enabling. It is five questions.

1. *Are they truly unable to do this for themselves?* "Carry each other's burdens, and in this way you will fulfill the law of Christ. . . . Each one should carry their own load" (Gal. 6:2, 5).
2. *Do you have the resources (time, energy, or finances) to spare?* "Anyone who does not provide for their relatives, and especially for their own household, has denied the faith and is worse than an unbeliever" (1 Tim. 5:8).
3. *Do they have skin in the game?* "When we were with you, we gave you this rule: 'The one who is unwilling to work shall not eat'" (2 Thess. 3:10).
4. *Will you feel cheerful if you say yes?* "Each of you should give what you have decided in your heart to give, not reluctantly or under compulsion, for God loves a cheerful giver" (2 Cor. 9:7).
5. *Is the outcome increased autonomy or increased dependency?* "The leech has two daughters. 'Give! Give!' they cry. There are three things that are never satisfied, four that never say, 'Enough!'" (Prov. 30:15).

However, as long as you are in balance, remember this principle: when we give of ourselves, expecting nothing, we receive much more than we ever thought possible.

We are to be generous and sacrificial in transferring relational nutrients to those who are in need. And we are to practice responsibility so that we can continue giving for a lifetime. Another helpful resource on the subject is *When Helping Hurts* by Corbett and Fikkert,[6] which provides a strategic path in this area.

CHAPTER 16

CHRONICS

Support without Enabling

I'm originally from the South, and a phrase you will often hear there about a person is, "Bless his heart." Though it can convey compassion, most of the time it means, "He is just not getting it." There is some reality he is not understanding or responding to.

And that, unfortunately, describes the chronic, which is a type of person who can be a significant nutrient drain on you. If you find you innocently keep pouring and pouring into someone, with no observable improvement over time, you may be investing in a chronic.

A chronic is best defined as an individual with four traits.

1. *Ongoing struggles.* The person is continually having some combination of problems with career, finances, marriage, family, parenting, emotional well-being, and physical health. These can continue for decades or sometimes resolve for a season and then recur again and again.

2. *Little insight regarding their part.* Chronics can hear advice from their friends over and over, but when it comes to understanding what part they played to get themselves into the situation, they blank out. They may be mystified, they may be upset with God, or they may see themselves as continually mistreated by others, but in any case there is little self-introspection.

3. *Dysfunctional behavior patterns.* It should be no surprise that chronics continue making the same mistakes and have little interest in insight. They have what is called a flat learning curve. It's a little like a three-year-old at dinner who throws her veggies across the room and gets a time-out from Mom. But when she is returned to the table, she throws them again. In her head, there is no connection between sowing and reaping.

4. *Harmless in intent but harmful in impact.* Chronics can be very kind and likeable people. They aren't malicious in their hearts. But, unfortunately, the effects of their choices on others can be seriously damaging: broken marriages, job failures, bankruptcy, struggling friendships, alienated kids. I have had lots of chronic friends (and I'm sure I went through my own chronic phase). I just have learned how to manage these relationships the right way.

Chronics and care individuals are similar in that they have significant ongoing struggles. However, a care individual is responsive to what she is given and takes responsibility for it, using the help and resources to change and grow. The chronic is somewhat of a black hole, with no change in sight.

A client of mine, Melissa, wanted to discuss her relationship with a friend, Andrea, about whom she was troubled. Melissa said, "Andrea is really struggling, and I want to know if I'm helping her in the right way." She told me that Andrea was a single mom who was having difficulties in several arenas. Her kids were constantly in trouble and acting out. She couldn't keep a steady job. She was depressed a great deal of the time.

"She does seem to have some significant problems," I said. "How long have these been going on? Six months? A year?"

Melissa said, "Nine years."

"That's a very long time. I respect your perseverance with Andrea. And it does take a long time to work out serious problems. Okay, what do you do to help her?"

"I meet with her for lunch once a week. I just listen to her, support her, give her advice, pray for her, that sort of thing."

"Those are good things," I said. "The real question here is, what does the growth curve look like for these last nine years?"

Melissa is a businessperson, and she understood quickly what I was asking. "Except for the fact that she trusts me and knows I care, it's a flat line."

"So the kids are still out of control, the job issues are not improving, and her emotional state isn't better?"

"Yes," she said. "I try to get her to go to a good church, see counselors, get an executive coach, and I even offered to pay for some of it. But she is always too busy with other things."

"And does she call you at night with emergencies and crises?"

"How did you know?"

"That's how it tends to work. Had you told me that over the last nine years, Andrea was doing significantly better, year after year, in parenting, career, and emotional health, I would have said things are going well. None of us have a problem-free life. But success in growth is that every year, we have different problems that arise from our higher-level positions and abilities. It's not like the movie *Groundhog Day*; we aren't stuck in the same repetitive struggles. The problems are different and based on successes.

"For example, with a reasonable growth curve, the kids aren't out of control but have some grade problems at school. She has kept a job for a few years, not a few months. It's not the perfect job, but it's in the good-enough range. And she is getting support from a healthy church and is regularly improving with a therapist. So though she still needs healing, her depression is not as severe as it was."

"So am I a failure as a friend?" Melissa asked.

"No, you're a very caring friend," I said. "You just have not been aware of how Andrea's mind works. She does not learn from experience; she keeps trying the same things over and over again, expecting a different result. And that is the definition of insanity. So she's a bit crazy in that regard. I also think that she doesn't use the relational nutrients you provide for her, at least not in a helpful way. A helpful way would be that when you listen to her and support her, she feels strengthened to persevere in difficult decisions, and when you give her advice, she writes down what you say. By the way, Melissa, how often in nine years have you seen her write down your advice?"

"I don't think I've ever seen that."

"Right. You are a very successful executive. I have seen people follow you around in your company, writing down what you are saying. But with Andrea, instead of taking notes on her cell phone, going home, and doing what you have suggested, she probably nods and says thank you and that's it.

"Unfortunately, you function as her antidepressant. You are warm, you care, and you listen. So she basically takes in the relational nutrient of containment, over and over, dumping her problems onto you. Then she leaves feeling loved and supported, and it lasts for a few hours. But she has not metabolized anything you gave her, using it to think or behave differently. She didn't burn up the fuel. So nothing changes."

Melissa was thoughtful. "Okay, the lights are coming on. So what is my part in this, and how can I help her in a more effective way?"

"Your part is that you didn't have the 411 on handling people who are chronics. You innocently thought and hoped that your care and advice would work, because that works with lots of people, yourself included. And you let it go on far too long before considering another route. You were just in what is called a defensive hope mode, waiting for things to get better based on hope and not based on reality."

Melissa nodded, taking it all in.

"I suggest this if you want to be a better friend to Andrea: The next time you guys get together, apologize that you haven't been helping her the way you think you should, and say you want to change things up a bit to make the relationship work better. This means that when you two meet and you give her advice, you want her to interact with you on the advice and work with you on whether she really thinks it will help and if there is a way she can tweak it to fit her better.

Make her a partner in her own growth, not just a taker. Then ask her to write down what specifically she will do to make the changes, and by when. Tell her you'll text her on the due date to see how it went and that you will be praying for her success."

Melissa added an "Uh-huh" and jotted a note.

"Then see what happens in the next few meetings," I said. "If she is getting things done and matters are gradually improving, keep going. If she is not following up and has lots of excuses, you may need to tell her that if she can't do what she has committed to do for her growth, you may need to meet less frequently, because it feels like the time is not helpful. You love her and will keep praying for her, but the face-to-face may decrease with no action steps on her part."

Melissa said, "She will be devastated if I do that. She has no other friends."

"We don't want to devastate anyone, but there is a reason she has no other friends. What if she's burned through everyone else because of her stance toward responsibility? Isn't it a favor to her to empower and respect her enough to give her a few chances to change how she does life?"

Melissa had hired and fired enough people in her career to understand this. It wasn't about becoming performance based instead of giving unconditional love. Melissa loved Andrea unconditionally and had proven it. And if she had to meet with Andrea only once every two months, that would also be unconditional love. No matter what would happen, she was not judging or condemning Andrea, nor was she saying that Andrea had to perform for love. She was saying, however, that Andrea had to perform for time. We are called to love people, pray for them, and be for them. But if people want our time, they need to be shouldering some of the burden, owning their lives, unless they are in the hospital, in hospice care, in a crisis, or barely surviving.

The narrative ended well, actually. Andrea was hurt but did agree to Melissa's terms. She knew Melissa's advice was good for her, and she was able to feel not only the antidepressant effects of the conversations but also the challenge aspects. Over time, as Andrea began making the right changes, Melissa was able to meet with her less frequently, which was okay with Andrea. She now had other sources of nutrients and was more independent and autonomous.

Look at a chronic as being the foolish person in Proverbs.

▶ "The waywardness of the simple will kill them, and the complacency of fools will destroy them" (1:32).

▶ "The way of fools seems right to them, but the wise listen to advice" (12:15).

▶ "A discerning person keeps wisdom in view, but a fool's eyes wander to the ends of the earth" (17:24).

▶ "Fools find no pleasure in understanding but delight in airing their own opinions" (18:2).

▶ "As a dog returns to its vomit, so fools repeat their folly" (26:11).

▶ "Stone is heavy and sand a burden, but a fool's provocation is heavier than both" (27:3).

We must never judge those with chronic tendencies. We all have our own inner chronic. Just realize that there is a definable and demonstrable pattern in the chronic, in that they are constantly struggling in major ways, have little interest in understanding their part, and have a flat learning curve.

Some chronics do change, as in Andrea's situation. And that is what we all hope for. Some take a very long time to change. And, unfortunately, some never change.

But your responsibility is to be in charge of how you are investing your time, energy, and resources. What I have found, especially in high-performing people, is that they are so optimistic, caring, and hopeful that sometimes they pour enormous amounts of themselves over years into people who have chosen not to burn the fuel and make improvements. So just ask yourself whether your nutrients are healing and changing things or you are a perpetual source of comfort to someone who will come to you again and again because you are caring but has no thought of using what you provide to help themselves.

Use the five-question matrix in the care chapter to determine whether you are supporting or enabling a person. The same principles apply to this category. Most of the time, when my clients use the information in this chapter, they begin to do some helpful pruning in their relationships and invest in better ways.

CHAPTER 17

CONTAMINANTS

Quarantine Yourself and Your Resources

I was getting some personal and professional historical information from Aaron, a new coaching client who was very successful in the tech world. One question I asked him, as part of my standard protocol, was, "What significant professional wins and losses have you experienced in your career?"

After reciting a number of great wins such as setting records in his company's performance, Aaron said, "The loss that shook me up the most, and I think I'm still recovering from it, is when my business partner and best friend betrayed me."

I asked him to tell me about it. Aaron and his best friend at the time, Nick, had started the company. Aaron took over the outward-facing aspects, such as sales and marketing. Nick covered the organizational structure, finances, and operations. They had a capital investor who partnered with them as well, with the three of them sharing ownership in the organization. The company grew quickly and was well respected in the industry.

After a few years, Aaron found that Nick had colluded with the investor to force Aaron out of the business. The contractual legalities were complex, but they had done this without breaking the law. On his part, Aaron had not protected himself well contractually, because he trusted Nick. Therefore a great deal of the relationship was based on a handshake and not documented.

Aaron was devastated. He lost his company, his business partner, and his best friend all at the same time.

When I asked Aaron how Nick justified all the harm he had done, Aaron said, "In public, Nick said that I was the bad guy. But when I met with him in private, he said, 'I just wanted the company.'"

I was floored at the brutality of Nick's statement. "That's the only justification?"

"That was it. He even smiled when he said it."

Aaron had to do his share of healing, recovering, and ultimately forgiving. It took him a very long time to trust other individuals. And he had to work through all the red lights he had overlooked with Nick, as he autopsied the relationship with me. Fortunately, he made a great comeback and is now doing very well. But the story illustrates the reality of the category of the contaminant, and the impact of this sort of toxic relationship.

A contaminant is one who seeks to harm others. It is a person who does not cause pain by accident or out of immaturity. That would be the path of the chronic. The contaminant is intentional in harming others.

Sometimes the motivation of the contaminant is personal gain, as with Nick. Sometimes it is revenge for a perceived slight. And in severe cases, the motivation is that harm itself is enjoyable.

Contaminants generally possess a deep envy of others, which they will often deny feeling. Envy is the stance of resenting the perception that all of the good is outside of oneself. They feel empty of being loved and graced themselves, and they experience others as possessing the good they do not have. The result is that they desire to destroy the good of others, whether it be a person's happiness, marriage, family contentment, business success, health, or financial well being.

Envy existed in the very beginning, at the fall. It is one of the hallmarks of evil. When Satan tempted Adam and Eve, he convinced them that God was being unfair to them when he didn't permit them to eat from the tree of the knowledge of good and evil. Satan said to them, "God knows that when you eat from it your eyes will be opened, and you will be like God, knowing good and evil" (Gen. 3:5). That is, God was insecure in his own position and wanted to keep humankind in their place.

Adam and Eve had basically won the lottery of all time. They had an ongoing relationship with God, each other's love, and a fulfilling and creative career. But because there was one no in the deal, they felt deprived, and envy won out. Adam and Eve's envy didn't control most of their major life decisions, so I wouldn't classify them as contaminants. But it was extremely destructive to themselves and our race.

The bottom line is that contaminants are more than just hurt people or misunderstood people or chronics. They are in concert with evil. They are the bad guys.

Contaminants are not just people like career criminals or mass murderers. Like Nick, they can be professional people. They can have families. And, unfortunately, they are in the church as well. They are not a high percentage of humanity and the church, but they are present, and I would guess you know that you have engaged with one or several of them. And we have to accept that they exist, and know what to do with them. Here are some suggestions that can help.

▶ *Love your enemies.* We must always default to love, as when Jesus said, "You have heard that it was said, 'Love your neighbor and hate your enemy.' But I tell you, love your enemies and pray for those who persecute you" (Matt. 5:43–44). We don't have an option. Seek their best and pray for them. That is what Aaron does regularly about Nick.

▶ *Protect yourself.* Do not expose your heart, time, money, or other resources to a contaminant, once their nature has been established. When it's time to shake the dust off your feet, do it (Matt. 10:14).

▶ *Tell them the truth.* Contaminants can change, though it takes a great deal of work on their part. But give them the relational nutrient of confrontation. Tell them about your concern over their behavior and path, express its impact on you, and warn them about what you are seeing that may be in store for their lives. Someone, or lots of someones, need to inform them, on a due diligence level.

▶ *Live in reality.* One of the biggest mistakes people make with contaminants is ignoring the negative because there are positives. It's as if because they have good traits, we should minimize the toxicity of the evil traits. It is what I call the "Hitler had a dog" reasoning. Never minimize this sort of wrongful character. You can put your life, assets, and family at risk.

▶ *Determine your actions by the fruits.* Only trust them when they have proven, objectively and over time, that they are trustable. And make sure you have input from safe people in your life about this, as it is often hard to be objective. Henry Cloud's chapter "The Wise, the Foolish, and the Evil" in his book *Necessary Endings*[7] is a good reference for further information.

Don't be discouraged by the negativity that contaminants exist. That will be a reality as long as the world endures in its current form. Just be informed, be aware, and keep good limits.

FIXING OUR COMMON PROBLEM

When I teach this material and then go into the question-answer period of the talk, the overwhelming response is, "Wow, I am so bottom heavy!"

The comment refers to the reality that they don't have a sufficient number of coaches and comrades, and even casuals, for health and success, and at the same time, they feel burdened by the amount of time they spend giving to care individuals, chronics, and contaminants. This leads to exhaustion, lack of energy, problems in priority and clarity, and lack of effectiveness.

This statement of imbalance does make sense, especially for individuals who are trying to make a difference in influencing people, whether that means running a Fortune 100 company, pastoring a large church, operating a small business, or raising great kids. There is a positive reason and a few negative reasons for this.

The positive is that you care about others and want to invest in them. People have all sorts of needs, and if you are a people-oriented individual, you know there is no shortcut to spending the necessary time and energy to help them grow, develop, heal, and succeed. Giving and spending ourselves is ultimately what we are called to do.

The first negative is that you may not have been aware that you, as a person yourself, have needs too and that you can provide only to the level that you have been provided for. You may have neglected your own relational nutrients. This then leads to not spending time with those who have them to offer, and not having them deliver them to you.

The second negative is that we often have a hard time structuring our relational priorities. It's difficult to say no to someone who is asking for your help, especially when you have the talents and resources to help them. So it becomes a problem of boundary failure.

The third negative is that the imbalance has a scope-creep quality to it. As in a business's creep, the bottom-heavy direction occurs gradually, over time. You just don't notice it's happening until you wake up and realize you feel drained dry and don't want to get out of bed and meet all the needs facing you in the office and at home.

Here are some suggestions that can bring you from imbalance to a good ratio of relationships. With that ratio, the transfer of relational nutrients works much better.

Add before you subtract. Something has to change. However, it is better to first add more of the top three categories than to begin by pruning back the bottom three. It takes fortitude and courage to cut back on relational investments, even if that means that you will need to meet less frequently with someone. It's always difficult. So you will need to bring people in who can provide you with the confidence and wherewithal to do that, or you are likely to end up in the situation you started with.

We are all busy people, so this may mean being a bit overbusy until you can start adjusting the bottom of the list. One idea, however, is to cut back on nonrelational activities that would be easier on you emotionally. That could mean internet, video game, or TV time that is more optional.

Quality before quantity. Take your time. Investigate the potential coaches and comrades in your sphere, and when in doubt, don't commit. We are talking about a lifetime change of relationships. Don't rush into this.

Care is not a problem. In no way should you perceive that care relationships are a problem. The best life is the one in which the only people you are investing in are those who need you. Remember that it is the time, energy, and resources that you don't have available which are the problem.

Calendar the life-giving relationships. What is calendared is much more likely to happen. Set these up and stick to them. Don't get stuck in the "I'll do it in my free time" thought pattern, which hardly ever works.

Get support for having the pruning talks. Make sure your Life Team knows the issues, agrees with your priorities and decisions, and supports your need to restructure your relationships. Have their voices in your head when you rearrange your seven Cs.

Remember that there are those who are self-absorbed and concerned only about their own needs. And there are those who neglect their needs and expend on others, only to live in an energy drain existence. Your own sweet spot is to receive well and give out just as well.

TAKE THE FIFTEEN-DAY RELATIONSHIP CHALLENGE

I want to introduce you to a good friend of mine, whose story exemplifies the ideas in this book. Mark Householder is president of Athletes in Action, an organization which uses sports as a platform to help people answer questions of faith. A ministry of Cru, AIA engages with athletes in the professional, collegiate, and other arenas to create vision, growth, and outreach to the world through the world of sports.

For the past several years, Mark has been exposed to and trained by the primary message of this book: people are God's fuel for growth. He has been deeply involved in the growth process and has committed a great deal of his and his organization's time and energy to this principle.

Mark will tell you that AIA's performance, its clarity, his personal life, his family, and his relationships have all been transformed by this idea. He has restructured how the organization operates, and it has borne fruit.

Mark once told me that one of the most profound insights he experienced in the process was simply that "we need to need," which I mentioned at the beginning of this book. Mark's leadership DNA was to be other centered, and he did not know how to recognize, respect, and provide for his own needs. The principles in this book provided a new, somewhat disruptive, but ultimately liberating reality. He and his ministry remain committed to and growing in this paradigm. They have made vulnerability a cultural norm in their individual, team, and larger meeting contexts, and the results have been transformational.

To help you begin to see visible results from applying this truth and the ideas mentioned here, I want to offer you a challenge. Starting with the Townsend Personal and Relational Assessment Tool (TPRAT), this quick (ten minutes) online survey will help you find out how you are doing in the four character capacities: bonding, boundaries, reality, and capability. It is free to anyone who purchases this book. After completing the assessment, you'll get a score of one to ten in each area, along with a customized report which lists your specific skills and gives you action steps to take to improve your scores and increase your personal growth.

Then, for the next fifteen days, begin each day with some time to think about how to take one or two of the action steps listed in your results. Whichever categories need attention—bonding, boundaries, reality, and/or capability—do the reading and complete the personal insight assignments step by step. Once you've worked through the chapters, it might take you a couple of hours to fully consider how best to apply the ideas. But assign yourself the task of considering specific actions you can take in one or more of your relationships to move them forward. And then, if you took note of some relationships that need attention as you read this book, go back and take those actions as well.

The best part is, once you've worked through all the insight assignments, you can take the TPRAT again for free to see how you've improved. When you see your score improved by the actions you've taken, you'll experience what so many others have reported, that recovering your energy for relationships is only one benefit of applying the instruction here. We are finding that people are encouraged with their growth upon knowing what to do and working on the skills. You will find the link and password to taking the TPRAT in the informational page in the back of this book.

It's easy to quickly read a book and feel like you've done something for yourself when you haven't. The transformational benefit you'll experience for a lifetime comes from taking the first steps. If you take the challenge and complete the personal insight assignments, you will gain significant growth from the new insights received and be enabled to begin making important life changes. Our brains store information much longer when we act on it. So begin to realize the benefits of this information in your life, and maximize the benefits for the people you care for.

You now know what the growth system for life looks like, why it exists, and how we bear good fruit. But each of us has a responsibility to consider who the right people are who can provide the right nutrients in the right quantities at the right times. In this way, we are regularly receiving and delivering what makes life work. Your task over the next fifteen days (or more, if needed) is to take steps to balance out with whom you should be spending more time, and which relationships you should be pruning back, so you can be fueled with the right ratios of nutrients.

Finally, let me challenge you to begin looking at your relationships in a fundamentally different way. Many of us see others as a burden we are to carry, personally or professionally. Or we see others as not all that interested in entering our wells. Neither of these viewpoints is entirely correct, and they're certainly not helpful.

Instead begin to look at all of this simply as an ecosystem created by God, in which your needs are significant for your well-being. And more, that there truly are others who would count it a privilege and an honor to provide you with the nutrients you need—certainly for your growth but also foundationally, because you are loved. Then pay it forward and transfer your own nutrients to those who need them.

That is the key for all of us, to the life that is well worth living. As Jesus said, "You did not choose me, but I chose you and appointed you so that you might go and bear fruit—fruit that will last—and so that whatever you ask in my name the Father will give you. This is my command: Love each other" (John 15:16–17). God picked you to go bear fruit, fruit of all kinds. And it cannot be done, in its fullest expression, without the love we are to have for each other, as it manifests itself in the giving and receiving of what ultimately are his nutrients for us.

God bless you.

EMOTIONS LIST

As I mentioned in chapter 3, you need to have a robust emotional vocabulary to provide others with the Q1 and Q2 relational nutrients. This list provides many of the words we use to describe feelings, and they are categorized for you.

Angry

- Aggressive
- Annoyed
- Disgusted
- Envious
- Enraged
- Frustrated
- Furious
- Horrified
- Irritated
- Jealous
- Judgmental
- Resentful

Anxious

- Agitated
- Apprehensive
- Desperate
- Dread
- Fearful
- Intimidated
- Nervous
- Panicked
- Suspicious
- Terrified
- Trapped
- Vigilant
- Worried

Confused

- Ambivalent
- Awkward
- Conflicted
- Insane
- Overwhelmed
- Shocked
- Stunned
- Unsure
- Unreal

Down

- ▶ Blue
- ▶ Burdened
- ▶ Dead
- ▶ Defeated
- ▶ Depressed
- ▶ Despair
- ▶ Disappointed
- ▶ Discouraged
- ▶ Helpless
- ▶ Inconsolable
- ▶ Hopeless
- ▶ Sad

Isolated

- ▶ Alone
- ▶ Avoidant
- ▶ Bored
- ▶ Detached
- ▶ Distant
- ▶ Empty
- ▶ Frozen
- ▶ Lost
- ▶ Numb
- ▶ Shy
- ▶ Unseen

Mistreated

- ▶ Abandoned
- ▶ Abused
- ▶ Attacked
- ▶ Condemned
- ▶ Controlled
- ▶ Humiliated
- ▶ Hurt
- ▶ Judged
- ▶ Misunderstood
- ▶ Rejected
- ▶ Smothered
- ▶ Unimportant
- ▶ Wounded

Positive

- ▶ Accepted
- ▶ Amused
- ▶ Attracted
- ▶ Brave
- ▶ Calm
- ▶ Carefree
- ▶ Cheerful
- ▶ Close
- ▶ Compassionate
- ▶ Complete
- ▶ Confident
- ▶ Connected
- ▶ Content
- ▶ Ecstatic
- ▶ Energetic
- ▶ Excited
- ▶ Free
- ▶ Friendly
- ▶ Grateful
- ▶ Happy
- ▶ Interested
- ▶ Intimate
- ▶ Joyful
- ▶ Loved
- ▶ Loving
- ▶ Passionate
- ▶ Peaceful
- ▶ Pity
- ▶ Powerful
- ▶ Proud
- ▶ Purposeful
- ▶ Safe
- ▶ Significant
- ▶ Spontaneous
- ▶ Superior
- ▶ Surprised
- ▶ Tender
- ▶ Thankful
- ▶ Vulnerable
- ▶ Warm

Self-Critical

- ▶ Ashamed
- ▶ Disqualified
- ▶ Failing
- ▶ Guilty
- ▶ Inferior
- ▶ Unlovable
- ▶ Worthless

ACKNOWLEDGMENTS

Sealy Yates and Mike Salisbury, my literary agents: Thanks for your belief in the ideas in this book, and your strategic partnership in making this all work.

David Morris, vice president and publisher for Zondervan trade books: Your commitment to quality publishing, and impacting the world by content in all its forms, is always an encouragement to me.

Mick Silva, editor for Zondervan: I have so enjoyed our partnership, and your competence in making the words flow helps and educates the reader.

The Townsend Leadership Group, led by Patrick Sells, Karen Bergstrom, and Fauna Randolph, and each director, consultant, and coach, as well as all of our clients and group members: Your expertise in developing high-performing leaders with a holistic paradigm has created a catalyzing partnership.

Scott Makin, executive director and cofounder of the Townsend Institute for Leadership and Counseling at Concordia University Irvine, Mike Shurance, dean of the School of Professional Studies, the faculty, administration, students, and alums: I'm so happy to be partnering with the competence and character of such a great team.

Maureen Price, executive director of Growth Skills, and the board of trustees, Jobey Eddleman, Mike Brock, Cakra Ciputra, Dr. Randy Rheinheimer, Pastor Vern Streeter, and Steve Uhlmann, as well as the workshop facilitators: You work miracles in the workshops and in the church, and are creating a movement of growth.

Dr. Henry Cloud: Thanks for all of your insight and partnership in the world of helping people and organizations become their best.

Christine Ames and Jodi Coker, my assistants: Your thoughtful and practical skills make everything work.

The Tuesday men's group: Our many years together make you "people fuel" in my life.

My advisory board: Thanks for your wisdom, guidance, grace, and truth.

Dave Lindsey: Thanks for your suggestion that I simplify the relational nutrients into categories, resulting in the four quadrants.

My clients and friends who have been part of this book: I have learned so much from being connected to you.

Barbi, my wife: Your constant support and advice is a lifeline for me.

Ricky and Benny Townsend, my sons: I love to see how you are carving out your own worlds in your spheres of influence.

NOTES

1. John Cacioppo and William Patrick, *Loneliness: Human Nature and the Need for Social Connection* (New York: Norton, 2008). "Our research in the past decade or so demonstrates that the culprit behind these dire statistics is not usually being literally alone, but the subjective experience known as loneliness. . . . Chronic feelings of isolation can drive a cascade of physiological events that actually accelerates the aging process. Loneliness not only alters behavior but shows up in measurement of stress hormones, immune function, and cardiovascular function. Over time, these changes in physiology are compounded in ways that may be hastening millions of people to an early grave" (p. 5).
2. More information is available at *https://en.wikipedia.org/wiki/5_Whys.*
3. Henry Cloud and John Townsend, *How to Have That Difficult Conversation: Gaining the Skills for Honest and Meaningful Communication* (Grand Rapids: Zondervan, 2015), 10.
4. "ICF Global Coaching Client Study," April 2009, *http://icf.files.cms-plus.com/includes/media/docs/ExecutiveSummary.pdf.*
5. You can find the article at *www.focusonthefamily.com/marriage/marriage-challenges/healthy-opposite-sex-friendships-in-marriage.*
6. Steve Corbett and Brian Fikkert, *When Helping Hurts: How to Alleviate Poverty without Hurting the Poor . . . and Yourself* (Chicago: Moody Press, 2014).
7. Henry Cloud, *Necessary Endings: The Employees, Businesses, and Relationships That All of Us Have to Give Up in Order to Move Forward* (New York: HarperCollins, 2011).

FREE ASSESSMENT TOOL
WITH PURCHASE OF
PEOPLE FUEL

The Townsend Personal and Relational Assessment Tool (TPRAT) is an online assessment designed by John. It takes 10 minutes and provides you with a 1-10 score on the 4 Key Capacities of Character:

| Bonding | Boundaries | Reality | Capacity |

You also receive a customized report with specific skills tailored to help increase your personal scores.

Go to **TPRAT.drtownsend.com** and use password: **PFUEL**

FREE RELATIONAL NUTRIENTS
DIGITAL QUICK REFERENCE TOOL

Based on the 4 Quadrants of Relational Nutrients material, you can download this simple chart onto your mobile device, to quickly identify which nutrient you need for today's challenges, or what someone in your life might need from you.

Click on **RelationalNutrients.com**

TOWNSEND INSTITUTE
FOR LEADERSHIP & COUNSELING

AT CONCORDIA UNIVERSITY IRVINE

Our academic arm, the Townsend Institute for Leadership and Counseling, at Concordia University Irvine, offers fully-accredited, relationally-based online degree programs which includes a Master of Arts in Organizational Leadership, Master of Arts in Executive Coaching and Consultation, and Master of Arts in Counseling. In addition, we offer grad level Certificates as well as Bachelor's degrees in both Leadership Studies and Organizational Psychology.

Go to **TownsendInstitute.com**

TOWNSEND
LEADERSHIP PROGRAM

In the professional development arena, The Townsend Leadership Program transforms leaders from the inside out, helping them hone both their professional skills and their people skills. TLP offers leadership training teams around the country led by directors who are personally trained by John. Available for those currently operating in leadership and influence roles. The program is a highly-structured and effective method to optimize leaders.

Go to **TownsendLeadership.com**